Learning To

Global Education 4–7

Susan Fountain

Stanley Thornes (Publishers) Ltd
in association with the World Wide Fund for Nature and
the Centre for Global Education, York University.

First published in 1990 by:
Stanley Thornes (Publishers) Ltd
Old Station Drive
Leckhampton
CHELTENHAM GL53 0DN
England

British Library Cataloguing in Publication Data

Fountain, Susan
    Learning Together: global education 4–7
    1. Infant Schools. Teaching
    I. Title
    372 1102
    ISBN 0–7487–0439–6

Typeset by Tech-Set, Gateshead, Tyne & Wear.
Printed and bound in Great Britain at The Bath Press, Avon.

FOREWORD

The approaches described herein will, I hope, serve as starting points for nursery and infant teachers who would like to become involved in the continuum of global education. Far more work remains to be done in this field at the infant level, such as exploring ways of integrating co-operative learning into the curriculum for children under seven, and in developing anti-racist and anti-sexist practice which is appropriate to the age-group. I hope this book serves as an encouragement to nursery and infant teachers to share, discuss, and create the materials and approaches for which there is such a need.

The use of 'she' and 'her' throughout the text is an attempt to encourage reflection upon the role of language in maintaining gender conventions and stereotypes.

ACKNOWLEDGEMENTS

I would like to acknowledge the support of the World Wide Fund for Nature in sponsoring the publication of this book. (Details of the Fund's Education Programme are to be found on p. iv.)

Many of the materials and activities described in this book were developed and trialled while I was a reception class teacher at the International School of Geneva, in fulfilment of the requirements for a Diploma in Applied Educational Studies from the Centre for Global Education at the University of York. I would like to gratefully acknowledge the financial support of the International School of Geneva which made this project possible.

Thanks are due to Gillian Leach of Battye St. Nursery School, Dewsbury, and Frances Woodward of Dunnington C. of E. Primary School, York, for allowing me to take photographs in their classes, and to Jenny Nutall of West Walker Primary School, Newcastle, for her examples of nursery children solving conflicts.

I am grateful to Claudia Merson, Margot Brown and Gail Slavin for their moral support. Geoffrey Crumplin also provided invaluable assistance with word processing. Finally and most importantly, thanks are due to the many children and teachers, too numerous to name, who have shared with me their feedback on these approaches.

Susan Fountain

The author and publishers are grateful to the following for permission to reproduce material: Sterling Publishing Co. Inc. for 'I Hug Myself 'Cause I Love Me So' from *Musical Games for Children of all Ages* by Esther L. Nelson. © 1976 Esther L. Nelson.

The World Wide Fund for Nature: Education Programme

WWF's Education Programme aims to develop resources which help pupils understand the world in which they live. This not only necessitates knowledge about the environment and the interdependence which links together all living things and the physical world, but also the development of personal skills whereby individuals can question, discuss, analyse and have the confidence to make informed and responsible decisions about the planet's future.

Parents and teachers have the challenging job of helping young people to develop feelings of worth, trust and self-confidence – personal qualities which allow more energy and attention to care for others. If, from the earliest opportunity, children can be encouraged to appreciate ideas of co-operation and sharing and to find solutions to problems through co-operation rather than conflict, they are more likely to develop the essential skills necessary to meet the environmental challenges that face the world today and in the future. *Learning Together* helps teachers in this process, providing strategies and practical classroom activities to foster self-esteem, communication and co-operation — skills which underpin all learning.

CONTENTS

CHAPTER 1   Laying the Foundations of Global Education   1
  What is Global Education?   1
  What Do these Concepts Have to Do with Young Children?   3
  Why Support Self-esteem in the Classroom?   4
  Why Develop Communication Skills?   8
  Why Promote Co-operation in Schools?   9

CHAPTER 2   Global Education Activities: Putting them to Work
            in the Classroom   14
  Personal and Social Education in the Nursery and Infant School 14
  Cross-curricular Topic Work   15
  Teaching the Core Subjects   16

CHAPTER 3   Approaches to Fostering Self-esteem   20

CHAPTER 4   Approaches to Developing Communication Skills   36

CHAPTER 5   Approaches to Promoting Co-operation   49
  Active Co-operative Games and Learning Experiences   49
  Co-operative Board Games   60

CHAPTER 6   Looking Beyond the Activities   75
  Classroom Implications   76
  Whole-school Implications   88

Bibliography   95
  Background Reading on Global Education and Child
      Development   95
  Practical Handbooks and Classroom Resources   96

Index of Activities   98

CHAPTER 1

Laying the Foundations of Global Education

What is Global Education?

'There are some people who want some land, and other people have it and they don't want to give it to them, so the people are going bang, bang, and all the houses are broken down. And all the cars are broken.'
A five-year-old's explanation of the conflict in Lebanon.

'That's silly! The driver can't be a *lady*!'
A three-year-old girl's comment when boarding a bus driven by a woman in the north of England.

'Is she going to starve there? I think she should take some food with her so she doesn't die.'
A six-year-old's comment on hearing that a classmate would soon be returning to her native country, Ethiopia.

'I didn't draw any black people because I'm a white person, and I don't think about black people.'
A seven-year-old's response to a question about his drawing of the multi-ethnic neighbourhood in which he lives.

'I'm going to paint a beautiful picture to send them so they can be happy again.'
A four-year-old's response to news of a volcanic eruption in Colombia.

Even in the early years of schooling, children try to make sense of the global trends and problems that their parents and teachers struggle with on deeper levels. The five children quoted above put into words their prejudices, as well as their caring, concern and empathy. There is a glimmering of awareness that perhaps they should *do* something about problems. They show that they are forming rudimentary conceptions, and misconceptions, about issues of peace and conflict, human rights, racism, sexism, global development and the environment. These issues, and the dynamic interaction between them, have been central to the field of global education as it has developed in Britain.

Just what sort of knowledge, skills and attitudes does global education aim to develop in children? Writers in the field (1) have identified several critical factors which are outlined overleaf.

1

Knowledge of interdependence: The concept of interdependence refers to the fact that the world today can no longer be thought of as a collection of distinct and isolated countries and groups of people, who live their lives totally separate from each other. There is no place on the planet that is not somehow linked to, and affected by, other places. In any town or locality, no matter how small or remote, we have only to examine the origins of the foods in the cupboard, read carefully the labels on our clothing, see where our children's toys are made, or consider the sources of the print and electronic media (TV, newspapers, video) which enter our homes, in order to realise the multitude of ways in which so-called 'foreign' places touch upon our daily lives. Consider, for example, the way in which shoppers in Britain become involved in the anti-apartheid movement when they decide not to buy South African produce; or the manner in which, in the late 1980s, the promotion of powdered milk for babies in South America led to a boycott in much of the Western world of products from Nestlé, a multinational corporation based in Europe. We are all undeniably linked to places we may never have seen.

An interdependence also exists between the previously mentioned issues (peace and conflict, human rights, etc.) in the field of global education. For example, the 1986 nuclear accident at Chernobyl was not only a major environmental problem; as a radioactive cloud spread without regard for national boundaries, the livelihood of sheep farmers in Cumbria was threatened, as was the life style of the Sami people of northern Scandinavia (2), thus raising questions of the violation of their human rights. Issues which may have once seemed unrelated are becoming increasingly interlinked.

Perspective consciousness: This is the awareness that our own perspective, our framework for thought and perception, is only one of many which are possible. Our perspective may not be universally shared, and potential for misunderstanding and conflict arises when we try to use our own point of view to interpret or evaluate the ways of life, behaviour or beliefs of others. Our perspective is shaped by, among other things, our age, class, ethnic group, gender, where we live, our occupation, language, religious and political beliefs, nationality and race; these factors may operate subconsciously to shape the way we see the world. Thus an action defined as terrorism by one person may be seen by another as the act of a freedom fighter struggling for liberation from oppression. Direct eye contact, considered a sign of friendliness and openness in one culture may be considered disrespectful or rude in another.

Developing sensitivity to other perspectives benefits children by helping them challenge ways of thinking and behaving which they may take for granted as 'normal'. It stimulates their imagination, promotes more creative thinking, encourages new ways of looking at problems and heightens respect for differences.

'State of planet' awareness: Children need to acquire an under-standing of present world conditions and emerging global trends. These might include, for example, equalities and inequalities in the distribution of wealth and resources; the positive and negative effects which humans have on the environment; and the existence of conflicts between groups of people and progress that is being made towards resolving these conflicts. They need to understand that there may be a range of conflicting arguments or points of view on these trends and conditions. They also need to develop a sense of what constitutes a healthy society: is a so-called 'developed' country really healthy when the wealth is concentrated within a small percentage of the population? Or when that wealth has been accumulated by promoting the growth of cash crops in 'less developed' countries, leaving fewer resources for growing food crops which are needed by the local population for subsistence? Or when the very industries upon which 'developed' countries depend threaten, through resource depletion and pollution, the well-being of the entire planet?

Awareness of human choices: Children need to learn that choices taken in one part of the globe simultaneously have an impact on other parts. The consumption of beefburgers in Great Britain, for example, affects decisions being taken to cut down tropical rain forests for grazing land in South America. Children also need to grasp that choices made today affect the future well-being of the planet. The use of ozone-damaging products today will affect the health of people in years to come. Failure to make choices and take action may have as much of an impact on the world around us as a consciously-made choice or act. Children need to see themselves as people who have the power to affect the world around them. Global education is ultimately education for action.

What Do these Concepts Have to Do with Young Children?

Conventional wisdom about good practice in nursery and infant education would suggest that the complex issues mentioned above are best dealt with when children are older and have achieved a greater degree of intellectual development. It is thought that children under the age of seven, who learn through their senses via first-hand experience of their immediate environment, cannot grasp abstract notions about justice, rights, resource distribution and interdependence.

Or can they? Not to the same degree as secondary school children, certainly; but in the course of the school day, in their relationships with peers and adults, young children do in fact have simple, concrete experiences which contain elements in common with larger world issues. The daily concerns of small children have parallels on the global level. Nursery and infant children regularly:

- Call each other names, sometimes gender- or race-related (prejudice)
- Exclude others from play for arbitrary reasons (discrimination)
- Argue over materials (resource distribution)

3

- Protest that rules are 'not fair' (human rights)
- Fight (peace and conflict)
- Use consumable materials, sometimes unwisely (environmental awareness)
- Find that by sharing and working together, more can be accomplished (interdependence)
- Negotiate to find a solution to a problem that both parties will find acceptable (perspective consciousness)
- Discover that some adults have power in the school to make decisions, or that older children may be allowed to do things that younger ones are not ('state of planet' – or in this case, 'state of school' – awareness)
- Decide what activities they will take part in: write letters, pick up litter, or plant flowers in the school grounds (awareness of human choice and action).

Such experiences, if sensitively discussed, will help young children begin to build an understanding of concepts they can explore in ever-increasing depth later in their schooling. Classroom relationships, whether conflictive or harmonious, possess at least as much learning potential as lessons in language or mathematics.

The learning *process*, as well as content, is essential to global education. Interaction is a dominant feature of junior or secondary classrooms where global education is in practice. Children work in pairs or small groups to encourage discussion, to air alternative perspectives, to negotiate and to make decisions; tasks are structured to encourage co-operation and participation by all; children examine their own points of view and attempt to understand those of others through the use of role-plays and simulations. Attitudes, values and feelings have as much place in such a classroom as 'factual' knowledge and skills. Emphasis is given to emotions, imagination and intuition, as well as to logical reasoning and analysis.

The early years of schooling are the beginning of a continuum in which such interactive techniques are developed and built upon. Nursery and infant teachers can do much to foster the social skills and attitudes which will lay the foundation for later work in global education. The three areas of **self-esteem, communication skills** and **co-operation** stand out in particular as ones which can be developed in young children. Strengths in these areas can help prevent inter-personal conflict, promote the peaceful resolution of conflict and encourage positive relationships and attitudes towards others. They can also prepare children to participate more effectively in the interactive learning strategies employed in the field of global education.

Why Support Self-esteem in the Classroom?

A healthy sense of self-esteem forms the cornerstone for constructive relationships with others. Children who view themselves in a positive light are more likely to see others positively as well (3). If children are to develop 'perspective consciousness', and the notion of respect and equality between different groups of people that should accompany that awareness, then a strong sense of self-worth is essential. Such a sense supports children as they take the risk of reaching out into new areas of learning, examining controversial issues and developing new or unfamiliar points of view.

A child's self-esteem is being developed throughout the day.

Poor self-image is sometimes cited as a source of inter-personal conflict (4), and there is thus justification for considering whether children who are particularly aggressive, or who have difficulties with peer relationships, may in fact be struggling to compensate for a low self-image. In some cases the need to disparage others through the expression of racist or sexist attitudes may arise in part from a sense of low self-esteem. However, this in no way excuses the teacher from the obligation to stop such behaviour immediately and to make clear to the child involved that it is unacceptable (nor does it negate the other complex social factors that may contribute to such behaviour).

It has been suggested that children who appreciate their own intrinsic value, and that of others, may in fact be less likely to tolerate discrimination and inequality, and more likely to take a stand against injustice (5). High self-esteem has been found to be linked, in older children, with a readiness to take action in the face of challenge or crisis, rather than with an attitude of despair or the expectation that someone else will solve the problem (6). For children who are aware of human choices, and of their own ability to act effectively in the world, therefore, self-esteem is vital.

5

A positive sense of self should be the birthright of every child; it is particularly important, however, that teachers should be aware of the development of self-concept in children who are members of groups who are discriminated against in any way. Their ability to cope with prejudice will, to a great extent, depend on their own sense of personal value. Research on the self-esteem of black children yields complex and often conflicting results (7); while some writers cite low self-esteem as a contributory factor to the underachievement of black children, others report no difference between blacks and whites in the range of scores on self-esteem tests. The latter suggest that the apparently well-meaning concern over the 'low self-esteem of black children' is in fact a thinly disguised racist attitude (8), which perpetuates the myth that black children have lower potential for achievement. Particularly risky is the attempt by white, monolingual teachers to assess the self-esteem of black, bilingual children about whose culture, language and home backgrounds they may know little. It is also worth bearing in mind that a lack of confidence in one particular ability (whether speaking English, playing football or doing Mathematics) does not necessarily indicate a low sense of self-esteem overall.

In the *process* of building self-esteem, sometimes referred to as affirmation, it is essential that children concurrently learn to identify and acknowledge the strengths of others. Encouraging students to value the contributions that peers make to the group has a particular importance in the early school years, when prejudices towards those of different ethnic and gender groups may not yet be firmly entrenched. If children can come to look at each other as individuals with unique positive qualities, rather than to classify each other solely by such labels as 'a black person', 'a girl' or 'handicapped', it is possible to break down narrow and restricting stereotypes before they become more rigidly set.

At a recent in-service training session on self-esteem held at a primary school in the north of England, teachers identified a number of behaviours which they considered to be characteristic of children who had a positive self-concept. These included:

- The ability to assess realistically both the strengths and weaknesses of their own work
- The ability to recognise the worth of others, and give affirming feedback to classmates
- The ability to accept constructive criticism and suggestions in an open-minded manner, without becoming overly defensive
- The ability to work co-operatively in a group, accepting the contributions of each member without needing to dominate or impose one's ideas on the others
- The ability to react reasonably and assertively in conflict situations, without relying on physical or verbal aggression.

This gives a useful picture of how a child with a positive sense of self functions. It is particularly interesting in light of the fact that some teachers express fears that supporting children's self-esteem will produce a group of self-centred, self-important students who have little consideration for others (attitudes sometimes thought to arise from having 'too much self-esteem'). An alternative point of view might be that such behaviour is an attempt to conceal the lack of a clear sense of one's own value. A body of research on children of all ages indicates that high self-esteem is associated with *less* egocentricity, rather than more; and with more altruistic behaviour, more sharing and generosity (9). Such characteristics are certainly among those one would hope to find in young people who are being educated to an awareness of global issues.

In addition to the positive effect of high self-esteem on social skills, there is increasing evidence of the benefits in terms of academic achievement. One study followed a group of reception class children until they were seven; in attempting to anticipate their success in learning to read, scores on tests of self-concept were more accurate predictors than IQ scores (10). In another extensive study of children aged between five and seventeen whose teachers had been trained to offer high levels of empathy and positive regard, students were found to have increased scores both on measures of self-concept and on Reading and Mathematics. Fewer disciplinary problems were noted as well (11). If high self-esteem positively influences both intellectual and social skills, then it seems essential that each child's daily classroom experience should include the receiving and giving of affirmation.

As teachers' awareness of the importance of children's self-concept grows, they often begin to use high levels of praise for positive behaviour. Certainly there is a place for this in the classroom, particularly for children who may arrive at school with such a poor self-image that they are withdrawn and unresponsive, fearful of making a mistake. Disruptive and aggressive children who seek attention in negative ways may also begin to flourish when given praise for constructive behaviour. However, excessive praise can become counter-productive:

> 'Lavishing praise indiscriminately . . . does not enhance self-esteem, but gives rise to suspicion about the motives of the praiser. True self-esteem comes from inside, from accepting our strengths, and is reinforced by an affirming and positive atmosphere, where we are encouraged to think positively about ourselves and build on our strengths.' (12)

There is a need for teachers to be honest with students; children intuitively sense when a compliment is insincere and may lose trust in an adult who does not relate to them in a genuine manner (13). Also to be avoided is the notion that children have 'no self-esteem' until their teachers 'build' it; such thinking leaves out the child as an active participant in the creation of her own identity. Work on self-esteem is likely to be more effective if it is thought of not as something a teacher does *to* a child, but as a process whereby the teacher supports the child in the continuing growth of her own self-awareness, and her ability to acknowledge both her own uniqueness and that of her classmates.

7

Why Develop Communication Skills?

Effective communication skills are fundamental to global education. The ability to listen, to absorb information and to question allows children to develop an awareness of how the world around them works, and of its important trends and conditions, whether local or global. Clear self-expression and the ability to listen with understanding are also the basic first steps to appreciating other perspectives.

The ability to communicate, particularly about one's emotions, may form a foundation for the exploration of ideas of fairness and justice. Once children can express what it feels like to be unfairly treated, they will have a reference point for imagining and understanding the reactions of others who experience injustice. The development of this ability to take the point of view of another, to understand their feelings and intentions, has been found to be a significant factor in the increasing maturity with which children make judgements about just and fair solutions to moral dilemmas (14). If concern for the rights of others develops earlier in children who can grasp what the feelings of others in unfair situations might be, then learning to communicate about the emotions may be the starting point for awareness of human rights.

It is not always easy for young children to identify and communicate their emotions appropriately.

Competence in speaking and listening is also essential to the prevention and resolution of conflict. The ability to express one's thoughts and feelings clearly is necessary in order to put forward one's point of view in a dispute; the ability to listen is obviously essential if one is to understand another's point of view. Children who can listen effectively and express their own feelings clearly are more able to solve social problems with peers: they more easily understand problems, suggest possible solutions, and anticipate the consequences of those solutions (15). Children who express their emotions effectively also show a greater inclination to give help to someone who is distressed (16).

Schools continually expect children to communicate what they *know*, but less often what they *feel*. This is especially so for boys, who in most Western societies receive persistent messages, both covertly and openly, that it is undesirable to display emotion. Happily, in their first years of school, most children have not yet fully mastered ways of meeting the societal demand to hide their feelings; emotions are still close to the surface. The early childhood years are thus an ideal time to help children learn to give names to their feelings, to explore the ways in which emotions are expressed, to distinguish between emotions which are satisfying and those which are uncomfortable, to share experiences that evoke particular feelings, and to try to anticipate what others might be feeling. Non-verbal communication skills of expressing oneself through movement and gesture, and the ability to observe and interpret those messages, can also be fruitfully developed by children under the age of seven.

As the development of communication skills relates well to the aims of the typical infant school language arts curriculum, work in this area may be relatively easy to integrate into the school day. It is vital to bear in mind, however, that the significance of these skills in terms of global education lies not only in helping children read, write, listen and speak more clearly; it also involves giving them tools that will foster social skills, improve their competence at negotiation and conflict resolution, enable them to begin to understand the perspectives of others, and encourage the growth of empathy.

Why Promote Co-operation in Schools?

Co-operative learning strategies allow young children to experience their class not as a collection of separate individuals, but as an interrelated system in which the actions of each member affect, and are affected by, the actions of others. By participating in such activities, they can, at a very early age, gain concrete experience of the highly complex idea of interdependence, which is so central to global education. A firm grasp of this notion in the immediate school environment can pave the way for a later understanding of the interdependent nature of relationships between ethnic groups and countries, of ecosystems, of world economics and of public health, to name but a few relevant areas.

Co-operative learning can have far-reaching implications for relationships within the class. Primary school children have been found to choose friends mainly from their own gender and ethnic group. But when placed in co-operative learning situations, the importance of gender and ethnicity in

9

choosing friends diminishes greatly (17). Co-operative learning, which is structured so that each child's participation is necessary for the group to succeed, allows all children to feel a valuable part of the group. It can thus help to break down the barriers of prejudice when used *consistently* over time, rather than as a 'supplement' to the curriculum on special occasions.

Unfortunately, a tendency towards competition often becomes evident even in nursery and infant classes. Work is frequently structured so that the individual completes tasks in isolation. Children helping each other are often thought to be cheating; there are few opportunities to learn together in a co-operative manner.

Competition in itself need not be seen as totally negative; for example, children may compete against an external standard, against the clock, or against their own past achievements. Competition can also be handled by adults in a more casual way than is often done, without glorifying or bestowing privileges on the winner, a practice which provokes the jealousy of the losers and escalates a cycle of more intense competition on future occasions. Competition which devalues and eliminates the 'losers' can be destructive both to a sense of individual self-worth and to group cohesiveness (18).

Co-operative games and learning experiences, on the other hand, build support and caring within a group. In co-operative activities, the stigma of failure is eliminated. The fact that players must work together as a unit, each having a necessary contribution to make, affirms the individual's self-esteem and sense of belonging (19).

One argument against the use of co-operative games and learning materials is that competitive games are superior with regard to the development of certain thinking skills:

> Since competitive games require rules, they offer special opportunities for children to engage in the making of rules . . . The goal of outdoing or outwitting an opponent provides a focal point around which the child is motivated to think very hard . . . In competitive games, children are highly motivated to decentre and plan strategies. (20)

It seems vital to point out that co-operative games also require rules. A co-operative game, because it involves all children fully, encourages them to comment on its structure, and to modify rules by a process of consensus, taking into account the feelings of each individual. The type of interactive classroom atmosphere which the use of co-operative games and learning experiences helps to create, strongly promotes the development of the ability to make rules; related intellectual skills such as role-taking, reasoning, devising alternative solutions and decision-making are also encouraged.

When children play co-operative games they *are* motivated to think very hard! Cognitive decentring (i.e. the ability to shift away from one's own perception of a problem and assume the perceptions of others) is indeed an important developmental task of childhood; trying to figure out what other people's moves might be with the aim of developing a strategy to beat them, might be one way of achieving this. However, in co-operative games children must decentre as well; tasks are designed so that they must take another person's point of view in order to develop strategies that will allow *both* their classmates and themselves to simultaneously achieve the goal. Players must use social and intellectual skills together, rather than in isolation, leading to what often appears to be a higher level of thinking than one finds in many competitive games for young children. Indeed, a wealth of research (21) indicates that achievement in all types of more complex thinking skills, such as concept attainment, problem-solving, categorisation and prediction, is higher when co-operative, rather than competitive learning strategies are used. Given a choice between an activity in which players decentre so that one person succeeds and all the others lose, and one in which players decentre so that *all* succeed, the latter seems to offer more academic potential, social benefits and fun!

Some teachers are concerned that an emphasis on co-operative work will not adequately prepare children for the demands of the competitive world in which we live. However, teachers need to bear in mind that today's students will, in the future, need the ability to work co-operatively with others to achieve common goals in almost any field of work they choose to enter. Indeed, schools have been criticised for emphasising an individualistic approach to work and failing to take into account the collaborative, sharing nature of most working groups (22). Even in highly competitive industries, there is an increasing trend towards co-operation and worker participation in goal-setting and decision-making (23).

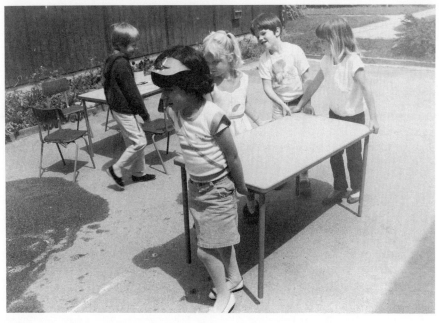

Working together co-operatively provides a concrete experience of interdependence.

11

Furthermore, the case can be made that escalating competition has in many ways led the planet to the brink of destruction. Competition for superiority in the arms race has led the superpowers to stockpile weapons capable of destroying human life many times over; at the same time budgets for housing, education and health fail to keep up with increasingly urgent demands. The race between multinational corporations for ever-increasing profits has led to the depletion of irreplaceable resources, while alternative energy sources remain largely unresearched. The effects of this type of competition on a global scale touch the lives of every person on earth.

If we continue to see competition as the preferable way of relating to others, we risk maintaining a status quo which threatens our very existence as a species. There is a need to redress the imbalance that presently exists in the many schools which only teach competitive approaches to problem-solving and fail to let children know that there can also be co-operative ways of achieving a goal. Rather than teach for the status quo, co-operative learning offers a way to teach for creative social change.

References

1 See for example, Pike, G. and Selby, D., *Global Teacher. Global Learner* (Hodder and Stoughton, London, 1988) p. 23. See also Hanvey, R., *An Attainable Global Perspective*, Global Perspectives in Education, (New York, 1976).

2 See Greig, S., Pike, G., and Selby, D., *Earthrights: Education as if the Planet Really Mattered* (WWF and Kogan Page, London, 1987) p. 4.

3 See Lawrence, Dennis, *Enhancing Self-Esteem in the Classroom* (Paul Chapman Press, 1987).

4 Prutzman, P., Burger, M. L., Bodenhamer, G., and Stern, L., *The Friendly Classroom for a Small Planet* (Avery Publishing Group, New Jersey, 1978) p. 35.

5 Cell, E., *Learning to Learn from Experience* (State University of New York, Albany, 1984) p. 24.

6 See the research of Helen Haste in 'Everybody's scared – but life goes on: coping, defense and action in the face of nuclear threat', *Journal of Adolescence* (to be published).

7 See Davey, A., *Learning to be Prejudiced* (Edward Arnold, London, 1983) pp. 85–91.

8 Stone, M., *The Education of the Black Child in Britain* (Fontana, London, 1981).

9 See Mussen, P., and Eisenberg-Berg, N., *Roots of Caring, Sharing, and Helping* (W. H. Freeman, San Francisco, 1977) p. 72.

10 Canfield, J., and Wells, H., *100 Ways to Enhance Self-Concept in the Classroom* (Prentice Hall, New Jersey, 1976) p. 3.

11 See research by Aspy and Roebuck, cited in Rogers, C., *Freedom to Learn for the 80's* (Charles E. Merrill, Columbus, Ohio, 1983) pp. 202–3.

12 Galloway, F., *PSE Teaching Pack*, Appendix three of *Personal and Social Education in the Primary School*, Diploma in Applied Educational Studies (University of York, 1987).

13 See Hitz, R., and Driscoll, A., 'Praise or Encouragement? New Insights into Praise: Implications for Early Childhood Teachers' in *Young Children* (July 1988).

14 Selman, R., and Damon, W., 'The Necessity (but Insufficiency) of Social Perspective Taking for Conceptions of Justice at Three Early Levels', in DePalma, D., and Foley, J. (eds.), *Moral Development: Current Theory and Research*, (Lawrence Erlbaum Associates, New Jersey, 1975) pp. 57–74.

15 Spivack, G., and Shure, M., *Social Adjustment of Young Children*, (Jossey-Bass, San Francisco, 1976) p. 37.

16 Mussen and Eisenberg-Berg, op. cit., p. 69.

17 See discussion of the implications of co-operative learning in Davey, op. cit., pp. 181–3.

18 Judson, S., *A Manual on Non-violence and Children* (New Society Publishers, Philadelphia, 1977) p. 49.

19 See Pax Christi, *Winners All* (Stanhope Press, London, 1980) or Orlick, T., *The Co-operative Sports and Games Book* (Writers and Readers Publishing Co-operative, London, 1978).

20 Kamii and DeVries, *Group Games in Early Education* (National Association for the Education of Young Children, Washington, D.C., 1980) pp. 197–8.

21 Johnson, D. W., and Johnson, R. T., *Learning Together and Alone* (Prentice Hall, New Jersey, 1975) p. 191. See also Johnson, D. W., and Johnson, R. T., *The Socialization and Achievement Crisis: Are Co-operative Learning Experiences the Solution?* (Sage Publications, 1983) p. 146.

22 Handy, C., *The Future of Work* (Basil Blackwell, 1984) p. 137.

23 Ferguson, M., *The Aquarian Conspiracy* (Granada, London, 1980) p. 36.

CHAPTER 2

Global Education Activities: Putting them to Work in the Classroom

The following chapters contain a range of activities for developing self-esteem, communication and co-operation skills in nursery and infant classrooms. The aim of this chapter is to suggest guidelines for integrating these activities into the curriculum. This can be done in three ways: by setting aside time during the day/week for **personal and social education;** by incorporating the activities into **cross-curricular topic work;** or by using them to give an interactive, co-operative dimension to the **teaching of the core subjects.** Ideally, all three approaches can be included in the school day. They are discussed in more detail in the following pages.

Personal and Social Education in the Nursery and Infant School

Rarely in schools for young children is personal and social education a timetabled subject, as it often is in secondary schools. Infants have times during the day which are designated for work on Reading and Mathematics, but not for the development of skills and attitudes necessary for life in a rapidly changing and increasingly interdependent world. Although most teachers of young children would like their pupils to understand themselves and get on better with each other, too many expect that positive social skills and behaviour will just 'happen'.

> '. . . there is probably no other area of the curriculum in which we hope for so much and yet teach so little.' (1)

An increasing number of teachers, dissatisfied with waiting and hoping, are setting aside a time each day, or several times per week, specifically for work on group skills and attitudes. These are often referred to as 'circle times', because activities are carried out with the group, teacher included, sitting in a circle. One aim of circle time is to provide a safe setting in which to express thoughts and feelings. Therefore it is important that certain basic

14

rules are established, such as: everyone listens to the person who is speaking, no one has to speak if they do not want to, no one makes fun of another person even if they do not agree with them. Exercises such as **Magic Microphone** (page 47) or **Bean Discussions** (page 48) are useful for establishing discussion skills.

Further activities can be selected according to the needs of the class. At the start of a new school year, introductory activities that help children to learn each others' names might be used. The group might spend circle time making and discussing **Affirmation Badges** (page 22) on the first day. On the second day they might try **Names in Motion** (page 44) as a way of learning each others' names. This could be repeated the next day to reinforce the recall of names, and the children could also play **This is my Friend** (page 20). The fourth circle time might be used for the **Introductory Name Game** (page 20), as well as a game such as **Doggie, Doggie, Where's Your Bone?** (page 56), a simple way of helping children begin to work together as a group. The last circle time of the week could be used for **Interviews** (page 21). Such a sequence of activities in the first week of school would go a long way towards helping each child to feel acknowledged and welcomed in her new class.

If the focus of circle time is to be listening skills, an introductory activity such as **Minute of Silence** (page 44) helps children become more attentive to sounds. **Pass the Sound** (page 41) requires still more focus on listening, without any particular attention to content. This could be followed by **Telephone** (page 36) and **Shipwreck** (page 57), which demand a greater degree of concentration and attention to the meaning of what is being said. **Overloading** (page 39) can encourage awareness of obstacles to effective listening; **Co-operative Storytelling** (page 46) allows children to use their listening skills to create a group product.

Each circle time should end with an opportunity for the children to evaluate: to say what they did or did not like about the session, what they feel they did well, what they could do better next time and what they have learned.

Cross-curricular Topic Work

Many of the activities described in chapters 3–5 can be used, some with slight adaptations, in the context of a class theme or topic.

Suppose an infant class has taken the topic 'Transport' for a term's work. The teacher may plan a range of activities such as:

- Using modelling materials to construct boats or wheeled vehicles
- Introducing a variety of toy vehicles into the construction area
- Conducting a survey of types of vehicles that drive past the school
- Turning the dramatic play area into a bus, an airport or a travel agency
- Making a graph to show how each child comes to school
- Taking trips to an airport, harbour, train station or garage.

15

In addition to such work, activities which build self-esteem, communication and co-operation could be included. Self-esteem work might include playing the **Introductory Name Game** (page 20) with questions such as 'How do you come to school?' or 'If you could drive any sort of vehicle, which one would you most like to drive?' **Interviews** (page 21) could be held in which children talk about a time they travelled by a form of transport they do not use every day, and what it was like. A page could be added to each child's **Affirmation Notebook** (page 29) on 'My favourite type of transport'.

Communication activities can also be geared around the theme. **Telephone** (page 36) can be played using messages about transport, such as 'Take the ten o'clock train to London'. **Pass the Sound** (page 41) can be played using the sounds of vehicles. **Escape from the Zoo** (page 42) can be adapted by assigning each child with the name of a mode of transport, with children changing place when their vehicle name is called, and everyone changing places when 'Traffic Jam' is called. A **Co-operative Storytelling** (page 46) session can be based on a transport scenario as well.

Co-operative games such as **Cars and Drivers** (page 55) will help children better appreciate the responsibilities of those who drive vehicles! **Shipwreck** (page 57) allows the whole class to share in that responsibility. **Co-operative Pin the Tail on the Donkey** (page 57) can be modified by using an outline of a car; children can give directions to their classmates as to where to place the wheels, windscreen wipers and steering-wheel. **Picturematch** (page 59) can be played using pictures of different vehicles, or by matching vehicles with pictures of their drivers (using non-sexist, multi-ethnic pictures). **The Bridge Across** (page 63) can also be used to promote discussion about transport across water, and the role it serves in bringing people together.

The activities described in the next three chapters could be incorporated into other topics as well. For example, the theme of 'My Five Senses' could use exercises which require listening, such as **Overloading** (page 39) or **Farmyard** (page 40) to make points about the sense of hearing; or activities involving non-verbal communication, such as **Telegraph** (page 38) or **Human Chalkboards** (page 39) could be used to supplement work on the sense of touch. **Affirmation Notebooks** (page 29) can be used as the basis for a topic on 'Myself'; suggestions on extending this topic are included in Chapter 3.

Teaching the Core Subjects

English, Mathematics and Science teaching (as well as Art and Physical Education lessons) can be enlivened through the use of many of the activities suggested in this book. Indeed, the development of self-esteem, communication and co-operation through these core subjects conveys the message that such skills are an integral part of school life, and not simply a pleasant change of pace.

English Attainment Target 3, for writing, states that children should be able to '. . . produce simple, coherent non-chronological writing' (2). This aim can be supported through the use of an exercise such as **Affirmation on Paper** (page 25), which not only requires coherent writing, but is highly motivating as well, since on completion of the activity each child receives a written testimony to her own self-worth.

Mathematics Attainment Target 10, on shape and space, states that children '. . . should recognise and use the properties of two-dimensional and three-dimensional shapes' (3). **Co-operative Circles** (page 72) and **Modified Co-operative Squares** (page 71) are excellent ways of achieving this aim. Not only do they provide plenty of experience with shapes in a problem-solving context, but they also promote the ability to share and work in a group at the same time.

Science Attainment Target 2 requires children to '. . . develop the knowledge and understanding of the diversity and classification of . . . life-forms' (4). **Co-operative Faces** (page 73) makes clear the diversity which exists among human beings in a positive manner, without the negative value judgements which are sometimes made when people are 'classified'; it simultaneously builds co-operation skills.

The matrix which follows (see pages 18–19) is intended as a quick guide to the activities described in this book, and the Attainment Targets for Key Stage 1 (levels 1–3) which they support. It shows that the development of personal and social skills need not be thought of as something external to the 'real' curriculum, but can be combined with the kind of cognitive learning that goes on throughout the school day.

References

1 See Cooper, F., 'Making Peace in the Classroom', *World Studies Journal: Global Education in the Early Years*, Vol. 8, No. 1.

2 DES, *English in the National Curriculum* (HMSO, May 1989).

3 DES, *Mathematics in the National Curriculum* (HMSO, 1989).

4 DES, *Science in the National Curriculum* (HMSO, 1989).

ATTAINMENT TARGETS	SELF-ESTEEM	This Is My Friend	Introductory Name Game	Attribute Linking	Interviews	Affirmation Badges	Mask Passing	Feelings Walk	Feeling Sounds	Affirmation on Paper	Police Officer, Have You Seen My Friend?	Body Tracings	The 'Seed' Visualisation	Affirmation Notebooks	I Hug Myself 'Cause I Love Me So!	COMMUNICATION	Telephone	Telegraph	Human Chalkboards	Overloading	Cooper Says
ENGLISH																					
1: Speaking and listening		●	●	●	●		●	●	●	●		●		●			●			●	●
2: Reading					●					●		●		●					●		
3: Writing					●					●				●					●		
SCIENCE																					
2: The variety of life		●	●	●	●		●	●	●			●		●							
3: Processes of life												●		●	●						
5: Human influences on the earth																					
10: Forces																					
14: Sound and music									●								●			●	
MATHEMATICS																					
2: Number														●					●		
3: Number																					
8: Measures												●		●							
10: Shape and space																				●	
11: Shape and space												●									
12: Handling Data			●											●							

ACTIVITIES

18

Column headings (reading left to right):

1. Farmyard
2. Pass the Sound
3. Listen and Clap
4. Escape From the Zoo
5. Minute of Silence
6. Names in Motion
7. Use Your Senses
8. Going Dotty
9. Co-operative Storytelling
10. Magic Microphone
11. Bean Discussions
12. **CO-OPERATION**
13. Musical Laps
14. Co-operative Musical Hugs
15. Co-operative Musical Hoops
16. Crowns and Statues
17. Class Web
18. Co-operative Hot Potato
19. No Hands!
20. Cars and Drivers
21. Doggie, Doggie, Where's Your Bone?
22. Shipwreck
23. Co-operative Pin the Tail on the Donkey
24. Lock and Key
25. Picturematch
26. The Magic Tree
27. Little Boy Blue
28. The Bridge Across
29. Building a House
30. The Park Game
31. Modified Co-operative Squares
32. Co-operative Circles
33. Co-operative Faces

Col	1	2	3	4	5	6	7	8	9	10	11	12	13	14	15	16	17	18	19	20	21	22	23	24	25	26	27	28	29	30	31	32	33
(shaded divider)																																	
R1	●	●	●	●	●		●		●	●	●		●	●	●	●	●			●		●		●		●		●			●	●	●
R2								●															●		●								
R3																									●								
(shaded divider)																																	
R4	●			●			●											●							●	●							●
R5						●	●												●				●										●
R6							●																						●				
R7																			●	●		●											
R8	●	●			●															●													
(shaded divider)																																	
R9													●	●	●			●								●	●	●					
R10																										●	●			●			
R11																												●	●				
R12																							●	●	●		●	●			●	●	●
R13													●			●	●			●	●		●	●	●	●	●	●	●	●	●	●	
R14	●		●	●														●								●	●						●

19

CHAPTER 3

Approaches to Fostering Self-esteem

The activities described in this chapter are designed to help children: feel positively about themselves; identify their own abilities and strengths; accept their emotions and express them in a constructive way; recognise the positive qualities of their classmates; make genuine affirming statements to others; identify what others might be feeling, and accept the validity of different emotional responses.

This is My Friend

Materials: None.

Procedure: The children sit on the floor in a circle. One child is chosen to begin. She introduces herself and the person sitting to her right: 'My name is Rima, and this is my friend Sarah.' The friend who has been introduced then continues, introducing *her* self and the person to *her* right: 'My name is Sarah, and this is my friend Tim.' Once the children are familiar with this procedure and each other's names, they enjoy introducing themselves and each person who has preceded them, so that the last child in the group has to recall all the names.

Potential: This is a useful game to play at the beginning of the year when children are learning each other's names. It reinforces the idea of friendship and the sense that everyone's name is valued, as well as developing listening and recall skills.

Introductory Name Game

Materials: None.

Procedure: The children sit on the floor in a circle. Each child in the circle says her own name and the answer to a given question, such as 'What is your favourite food?' 'What do you like best in school?' (The questions for young children need to be kept fairly simple and concrete.) Once children have some experience of introducing themselves in this way, they can try repeating the response of the person before them, followed by their own. Slightly older children may later move on to repeating the responses of all the children who have preceded them.

Potential: This is an excellent exercise in listening and remembering. Commonalities in responses to the questions can be pointed out as a way of encouraging the children to identify with each other, but children should be affirmed for their uniqueness and originality as well.

Source: Basic format first published in Prutzman et al (see Bibliography).

Attribute Linking

Materials: None.

Procedure: An attribute – a quality or characteristic – is chosen by the teacher, who calls it out. Children then walk around the room to join up with all the others who have the same attribute as themselves. For example, if the teacher calls out 'Favourite Colour', the children move around the room saying their favourite colour repeatedly, and linking arms with others who are saying the same colour, to form a group. As new attributes are called out, the groups break up and new groups are formed. Other attributes could include favourite animals, foods, means of travel to school, pets, types of clothing worn, television programmes watched.

Potential: A simple and lively way to experience being affirmed as part of a group and to discover attributes in common with other class members. This exercise could be used as part of a Mathematics lesson on sets, classification or grouping.

Source: Basic format first published in Pike and Selby (see Bibliography).

Comment on **Attribute Linking** by a teacher of six-year-olds:
'I think that A. and B., who are always fighting with each other, were surprised to find that they had some things in common! They were together in two groups; they both had the same favourite sport (snooker) and the same kind of pet (a budgie).'

Interviews

Materials: None.

Procedure: The group decides on one question that will be the topic of the interview. Any of the following could be used:
What makes you feel happy?
What makes you feel sad?
What do you like best about this class?
How do you know when someone is your friend?
What do you do to be a good friend?
The children split up into pairs and interview each other starting with the chosen question. They can then report their partner's responses to the whole group. This can be done effectively in 'chat show' style, by having pairs sit in

two chairs facing the group, or behind a low table, as is sometimes done on television. The interviews can be tape-recorded, or better still, recorded on video.

Potential: A useful exercise in the context of the English curriculum which develops the ability to formulate questions, give focused responses and recall information. It is also an excellent way of helping children to get to know each other. As there are no right or wrong answers to the questions, all children can feel affirmed by the process. Creating a setting with chairs or a table helps children take their speaking roles more seriously and creates a focus for the attention of the audience. Seeing oneself on video is particularly affirming at this age; it is also interesting to play back the video later in the year and encourage children to try to assess ways in which they have developed or changed. Would they give different responses to the questions now than they did the first time? Would their responses be longer and more complex? Has there been a growth in confidence in speaking, particularly for those who are learning English? Giving children the opportunity to reflect on the ways they have developed over the course of the year is an important esteem-building experience.

Affirmation Badges

Materials: Plain badges with pins, or self-adhesive address labels. Felt-tip pens.

Procedure: Each child is given a badge or label to decorate as she chooses. There are a variety of ways of doing this. Children may write their name and draw a picture of themselves, of something that they like, or something they enjoy doing. They may draw a face or an abstract design that expresses how they are feeling at that moment. Older children may write their name and a positive adjective beginning with the same letter as their name, for example, 'Smiling Sarah' or 'Amazing Ali'. After completing their badges, children can walk around the room, look at each other's badges, and discuss them.

Potential: An affirming activity that each child can do at her own level – there are no 'wrong' responses. It is also an enjoyable way of introducing the concept of adjectives, or initial letter sounds. Children will enjoy wearing the badges all day.

Mask Passing

Materials: None.

Procedure: The children sit on the floor in a circle. One child is chosen to make a face which expresses a particular emotion, and she then 'passes' it to the person sitting next to her. The second person imitates the facial expression and passes it along to the next child. Once the mask has gone around the circle, the children can guess what the emotion being expressed was.

Variation: Once children understand how to pass the mask, they can go on to imitate and then transform the facial expression as it is passed on, so that it changes with each succeeding child.

Potential: A way of helping children identify and label the range of emotions they feel, to develop observation skills, and to begin to explore non-verbal communication.

Feelings Walk

Materials: None. A hall or large space with room for moving around.

Procedure: An emotion is chosen – happy, sad, angry, frightened, surprised, proud, silly – and children walk around the room in a way that expresses this emotion. They can also try isolating one body part at a time and making it express the emotion: 'Move your head as if you're angry' or 'Move your hands as if you're scared'. Another possibility is to play a simple guessing game by having one child move while the others try to guess what emotion is being expressed.

Potential: A way to further extend exploration of non-verbal communication. The exercise can help children feel safe and affirmed in expressing their feelings physically and identifying what emotions others might be expressing through their bodies. It also helps them to learn that there are words that describe these emotions. Follow-up discussions can focus on what situations make them feel happy, sad, angry, proud or frightened; this exercise can be used as a basis for creative writing.

Feeling Sounds

Materials: None.

Procedure: An emotion is chosen – happy, sad, angry, frightened – and the children together make a sound which expresses that feeling. This can also be done as a guessing game, with one child making a sound and the others trying to guess what feeling is being expressed; it is even more effective if the children who are guessing keep their eyes closed while they listen.

Potential: Another way of helping children to express and identify a range of emotions in a non-threatening context, while developing listening skills.

For The Reading Corner

Jack and Jake by Aliki (The Bodley Head, 1986). No one seems to be able to tell twins Jack and Jake apart. Finally their sister sets the confused adults straight in this humorous story which affirms the uniqueness of each individual's identity.

23

Sally Ann in the Snow by Petronella Breinburg (The Bodley Head, 1977). Sally Ann is a young black girl who watches the other children sledging, but is afraid to have a go herself. She finally overcomes her fear at the end of the story in a surprising way. A useful book for stimulating discussions about fears and the satisfaction that comes from learning a new skill.

Oliver Button is a Sissy by Tomie de Paola (Methuen, 1981). A boy who prefers dancing and dressing up to football and basketball is teased by classmates at school. But his tap-dancing performance in a school talent show earns him the admiration of his friends and family alike. An up-beat story about having the courage to be who you really are.

Titch by Pat Hutchins (The Bodley Head, 1978). Titch is always too small to keep up with the games his older brother and sister play, until at the end of the story they realise that he has a unique and indispensible contribution to make. A springboard for discussing feelings of rejection and inclusion with very young children.

Tariq Learns to Swim by Hassina Khan (The Bodley Head, 1983). Tariq feels lonely and left out at school – until he learns to swim. His new-found skill helps him build his self-confidence and he ultimately finds his place among his friends.

Overnight Adventure by Frances Kilbourne (The Women's Press, 1977). Two girls spend the night in a tent, braving a variety of imagined dangers, and ultimately falling asleep! Delightfully told without words, a story of surmounting childhood fears.

I Wish I Could Fly by Ron Maris (Puffin, 1986). A turtle wishes he could do all the things his animal friends do – fly like the bird, run like the rabbit. But in the end he discovers that he can do something none of the other animals can do. Appropriate for nursery children.

I Was Only Trying to Help by J. J. Strong (Bell and Hyman, 1984). Kate, aged six, tries to help around the house, but only seems to create chaos. When she retreats to her room to suck her thumb, her parents reassure her that they know she was only trying to help. A story that many young children will empathise with!

The Girl With No Name by Ruth Thomson, 'The Rights of Children' series (Basil Blackwell, 1978). This book, one of a series which covers each item in the United Nations Declaration of the Rights of the Child, deals with a nameless girl who is discovered floating on an iceberg. She is never really happy in her adopted country – until her own family is found at last and she is able to speak her own language and use her real name. A way to raise issues about important elements of one's identity.

I Can Do It! by Shigeo Watanabe (Puffin, 1981). For very young nursery children, this simple book shows Little Bear determined to ride a bicycle, roller-skate, and even drive a bus – by finding his own unique ways of doing so. Young children will respond to Bear's need to feel competent and successful.

Affirmation on Paper

Materials: A sheet of A4 paper and a pencil for each participant.

Procedure: Participants sit in a circle in groups of six to eight. Each person writes her name on the bottom of her sheet of paper. She then passes her paper to the person on her right. Each person in the circle now has a paper with someone else's name on it. At the top of the paper everyone writes an affirming word, phrase or sentence about the person whose name appears at the bottom, and then folds the paper over so that the line of writing is concealed. Papers are then passed on to the right, and the procedure is repeated. When the papers reach their original owners they are unfolded and read silently. Then one at a time, each participant reads out what is on her sheet, preceding each line with the words 'I am . . .'

Potential: A highly affirming activity for children who can read and write, which could be incorporated into a writing exercise. Those who have difficulty writing should be allowed to use pictures as well. Children often save and treasure these sheets.

This is also a highly effective technique for use in in-service work. For adults, reading aloud the affirming comments made by others can cause feelings of embarrassment; a frequent experience is that it is easier to give affirmation than to 'own' it. Participants should be given time to fully discuss how they reacted to the exercise and why.

Source: Basic format first published in Masheder (see Bibliography).

Comment made by a seven-year-old three months after doing **Affirmation on Paper** in class:
'I saved my paper in my dresser drawer at home. Sometimes when I'm feeling sad, I take it out and look at it.'

Police Officer, Have You Seen My Friend?

Materials: None.

Procedure: Two children are selected from the group; one plays the role of a police officer and the other is a child who has lost a friend. The latter child decides who in the group is going to be the lost friend, but must not tell anyone. She then describes the lost friend to the police officer, using only positive qualities: what she likes about her, what she is good at doing, ways she is helpful or friendly. (If necessary, the police officer can ask a few questions.) Based on this description, the police officer has three guesses in which to identify the lost child. If she cannot solve the problem, other members of the police department (the rest of the children in the class) may be called upon to assist.

Potential: An excellent way of building descriptive language, this game is a great favourite of children under the age of seven (and many older children as well!). There may be a tendency to describe each other's physical characteristics at first, but with practice they will become more adept at identifying and affirming each other's personal qualities. Care should be taken not to use the sexist term 'policeman', and to see that both boys and girls have the opportunity to be the police officer.

Source: Basic format first published in Borba and Borba (see Bibliography).

Body Tracings

Materials: Large sheets of paper; paints and/or collage materials.

Procedure: Each child lies down on a large sheet of paper, and has her silhouette traced by the teacher or another child. The children then use paint and/or collage materials to fill in the shapes, making life-sized self-portraits.

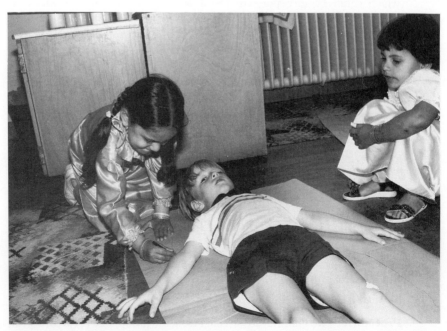

*Making **Body Tracings** requires concentration.*

Variations: The body tracings can be hung around the room. Children can write (or dictate to an adult) affirming comments about each other, and these can be hung beneath the pictures as captions.

Another variation is for two children to hold hands and lie down together on a very large sheet of paper. They can be traced around as if they were one, creating a 'double silhouette'. They can then work together to decorate their outlines. This can be followed by writing a few sentences on 'Why we are friends' or 'Why we like each other.'

Potential: A way to introduce self-esteem work into the Art period, which results in a most effective classroom display. This is an ideal activity to use as part of a topic on 'Myself' or 'Friends'. Having children make captions about each other encourages them to identify each other's positive qualities.

The 'Seed' Visualisation

Guided visualisations, or guided fantasies, can be a useful way of developing intuition, empathy and sensitivity to feelings, creativity and mental imagery, faculties which do not always receive as much attention in schools as do reasoning and analysis. Before attempting as lengthy a visualisation as the one described below, children should have some experience with simple relaxation exercises, such as **Minute of Silence** (page 44), or the exercise of tensing and relaxing one part of the body at a time (toes, legs, stomach, chest, fingers, arms, shoulders, neck). Very simple visualisations can then be tried, such as imagining floating on a cloud in the sky, or being a butterfly moving slowly from one flower to the next. As the time increases during which they can remain quiet and focused, more complex visualisations can be attempted.

Materials: A large open space in which children can lie down without touching each other. Optional: quiet background music; paper and drawing materials.

Procedure: The children lie on the floor in a comfortable position; relaxing music may be played in the background. The teacher asks them to close their eyes and listen to the following story, trying to see the pictures in their minds. The story is read in a clear but quiet voice, with frequent pauses to allow the children time to create their mental pictures (the reading of the visualisation below should take about ten minutes).

> Imagine you are a seed, a beautiful seed . . . What colour would you like to be? . . . What shape would you be – round? . . . square? . . . pointy? . . . What size would you be? . . .
>
> Now imagine that someone who loves you picks you up in their hand very gently . . . and puts you in a special spot in the ground . . . It's a place that's very soft and warm and safe . . . Now you're deep in the ground, waiting to be ready to grow . . .
>
> That person who loves you comes every day to take care of you . . . That person gives you water . . . and makes sure no weeds grow around

27

you . . . That person always makes sure you're warm enough . . . And sometimes that person even talks to you softly, and sings songs to you . . .

One day when the time is right, you begin to grow . . . You feel yourself pushing out of your seed coat, because it's too small for you now . . . And you begin to grow up, out of the warm, dark earth . . . Do you grow slowly? . . . or quickly? . . .

Finally you begin to push your way up into the sunlight and the fresh air . . . And as you grow, you become a very special plant, strong and healthy . . . exactly the sort of plant you are supposed to be! . . . Imagine what you look like as a plant . . . Are you tall? . . . short? . . . or in-between? . . . Do you grow straight up? . . . Or out to the side? . . . Or in both directions at once? . . . What colours are you? . . . Does anything grow on you – leaves? . . . fruit? . . . flowers? . . . or something else? You can have anything at all growing on you, because you are a very special plant . . . Are you close to any other plants, or all on your own? . . . Do any animals come near you? . . . If so, what do they do? . . . Do any people come near you? . . . If so, what do they do? . . .

Now imagine that a beautiful garden has grown up all around you, full of other plants, all different and all beautiful . . . There's a path through this garden, and it leads right to the beautiful plant that is you . . . Now it's time to step out of your special plant and take a good, long look at it . . . Try to remember exactly what it looks like . . . What does your plant need to keep on growing and becoming more special? . . . When you know what it needs, imagine that you're giving those things to your plant . . . When you've done that, you can begin to walk slowly down the path . . . The path leads right back into this room, so any time you want to go back to the garden to see your special plant, or to take care of it, you can just follow this path again . . . But now it's time to come back to this room, so follow the path until you get here . . . And when you get here, you can open your eyes.

The children who wish to share their visualisation can describe the experience to the group. (Some children may not wish to participate in such a discussion, owing to the personal nature of the visualisation, and should not be required to do so.) Questions to guide the discussion might include:
What did you look like as a seed?
What did the person who took care of you do for you?
How did it feel to be under the ground?
How did it feel to be growing?
What did you look like as a plant?
Which did you enjoy being most, a seed or a plant, or both?
What are the good things about your plant?
What things did you do to take care of your plant before you left the garden?

Variation: Some children may enjoy drawing pictures of their seeds or their plants. However, the emphasis of the experience should be on the imagination process, not on creating a tangible product.

Potential: An experience that allows children to develop positive, ideal images about themselves in a safe and private context. It has also been used in the context of science topic work on plants, to help children imagine what the growing process is like.

Comments by a group of five-year-olds on **The 'Seed' Visualisation:**
'I liked being in the ground best of all.'
'When I was growing I felt like a big beanstalk.'
'I had a beautiful flower, with a butterfly sitting on me.'
'I made a fence around my plant, so no rabbits could eat me up!'

Affirmation Notebooks

Materials: Sheets of A4 paper with headings as described on the following pages; crayons, pencils or felt-tip pens.

Procedure: Children fill in sheets (as illustrated on the following pages) by completing the sentences, or dictating their ideas to an adult if they are not yet old enough to write. They can add pictures where appropriate and colour or decorate their pages as they like. When all the pages are completed, they are assembled between two sheets of coloured paper which form a cover, and the child can write the title, 'A Book About Me'. Self-portraits, hand prints, foot-tracings or drawings can also be used to decorate the cover. Work on the books could form the focus of a term's work on 'Myself', with related activities planned in other areas of the curriculum. The following are some suggestions for **Affirmation Notebook** pages, with follow-up activities where appropriate.

My Name is . . . The children first write in their name and then their age on the line that says 'I am ____ years old.' They complete the page by drawing a picture of themselves. Having a mirror available as they do this is helpful. A number of activities could follow work on this page. In Art, painting a large self-portrait, or making **Body Tracings** (see page 26) would be appropriate at this point. As there is often almost a year's difference in the ages of the children within a class, an ages graph can be made showing, for example, how many in the class are five, and how many are four years old. This in turn often leads to a discussion of when each child's birthday is, an appropriate topic for another graph: How many people have birthdays in October? In November? In December?

There are . . . people in my house The children write in the number of people who live at home with them and then draw a picture of each person. Young children sometimes will not be able to determine how many people there are until they have drawn them. Teachers should be aware that some children may not live with certain members of the traditionally-conceived nuclear family, and may draw persons to whom they are not related. Others may include aunts, uncles, cousins, grandparents and other members of the extended family. Some children will want to include pets if they have them. If building self-esteem is the aim of the exercise, then it is

29

important to accept responses on this sheet without judgement. Another graph would be a logical follow-up activity: How many children have two people living in their house? Three? Four?

These are things I like to do The sheet shows a cluster of four balloons on strings. For older children, writing one thing they like to do inside each balloon makes an attractive presentation. For younger children, this may be

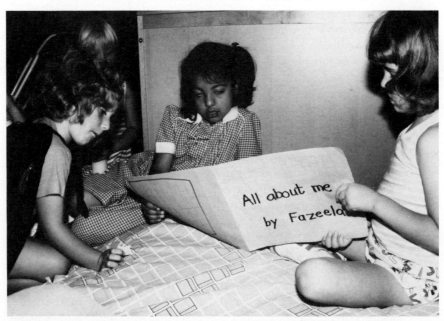

Affirmation Notebooks *belong in every classroom reading corner.*

too much writing in a small space. A sheet which says, 'At home, I like to ____' and 'At school, I like to ____' followed by a blank space of approximately half the page, allows the children more space to write and draw pictures of their favourite activities. It is important to discuss this sheet once it is completed, noting similarities between children's responses where they occur. Children can be asked to walk around the room with their sheets and try to find another person or a group of people who have the same interests.

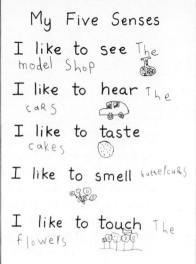

My Five Senses The children complete the sentences: 'I like to see . . .', 'I like to hear . . .'. In a topic on 'Myself', science work could be developed around each of the five senses. Young children are endlessly fascinated by the workings of their own bodies, and are eager to find answers to such questions as 'What is inside the ear?' and 'Why do some things taste good and others taste bad?'. Reading the pages on the senses aloud to the class can be particularly useful for provoking recognition and acceptance of individual differences. The children are often amazed to discover, for example, that one person's favourite food may be exactly that which is most disliked by someone else!

My hair is . . . The children try to determine the colour of their hair, skin, and eyes, and complete the corresponding sentences. Young ones often need the help of a mirror. In an ethnically mixed class, graphs can be made of eye, hair and skin colour, and the attitude that diversity in physical appearance is accepted and valued can be conveyed. This could be incorporated into science work on the variety of life. (In a class where Asian or Afro-Caribbean children form a small minority, however, such graphs may reinforce feelings of being different and isolated, and would therefore

be inappropriate.) The final sentence reads 'I am as tall as . . .'; there are a number of possible ways to complete this, depending on the age of the class. They may find another child of the same height and fill in that child's name; they may find an object of the same height in the room, and write its name ('I am as tall as the teacher's chair.'); they may work in pairs to measure each other with some non-standard unit, such as a building block ('I am as tall as 12 blocks.'); or they may use rulers and work together to measure each other. A bar graph, made by cutting a separate strip of paper to the height of each child and lining them up in order from shortest to tallest, is an effective follow-up.

I feel happy when . . . On this page there are three blank 'faces' (circles). The first two have the captions 'I feel happy when . . .' and 'I feel sad when . . .'. The children draw a happy and a sad face on the first two circles. On the third, they draw a face expressing another emotion of their choice. They then write or dictate about what makes them feel happy or sad (or scared, angry, proud, silly). Reading these pages aloud provokes worthwhile discussion – children remark that the same situation makes them feel the same way, or differently. A foundation for developing empathy and understanding of other points of view can be laid here.

If I could have one wish come true . . . The children complete the sentence and draw a picture of what they would wish for. This can offer insights into more private areas of a child's life. When reading these pages aloud the children can be encouraged to empathise with each other by asking, 'Has anyone else ever wished that? Why?'

Here are my friends The children draw and label pictures of their friends. Often they draw those who they would *like* to have as their friends. This activity prompts discussion of what it means to be friends. Responses of children under seven commonly tend to be very concrete: a friend is someone who plays with you, who shares their food or toys with you, who helps you if you have a problem, or invites you to their house. A useful follow-up to this page is the activity **Class Web** (page 53).

Here are some things we like about . . . On this page, other children write or dictate comments about their classmate whose name appears at the top of the page. The child who is the subject of the page can choose who to ask for comments, or names can be selected at random. This is a highly affirming activity and well worth the time spent on it.

Here are some things we like about Isabel:

Louise says "Isabel is kind"

Edward says "Isabel builds good castles"

Rupert says "I like playing Lego with Isabel"

I'm glad to be me because

I like my toys.
I like my house.
I like building.

> Some sample comments made by reception class children in their classmates' **Affirmation Notebooks:**
> 'I like playing with her because she is quite nice to me.'
> 'I like him because he invited me to his house.'
> 'I like her because she always waits for me on the steps.'
> 'He helps me in the building corner.'
> 'You are very kind to me.'
> 'I liked when you share your snack with me.'
> 'You make beautiful paintings.'
> 'I like playing outside with you.'

I'm glad to be me because . . . This makes a very satisfying final page for an Affirmation Notebook. Young children may have some difficulty with it, as it is not a type of statement they are often asked to make. For this reason, it is helpful to have this page follow the one in which other children point out some of the child's positive qualities. Again, responses tend at first to be concrete and immediate ('I like my toys'), and it may require some encouragement to help children reflect on their own personality and characteristics.

Potential: The making of Affirmation Notebooks is a well-tried technique for fostering a positive self-concept. Pages can be selected which allow children to meet a range of English, Mathematics and Science skills objectives. With the completion of the book, each child has a deeply valued, unique and personal product to share with the class and her family.

> Parents' comments upon reading their children's **Affirmation Notebooks:**
> 'This is something we'll always save to remember this year by.'
> 'I really learned something about how my child feels when I'm away on business.'
> 'I loved reading the part about the other kids' comments. It's interesting to see your own child through other children's eyes.'
> 'You must have a lot of fun in this class!'

I Hug Myself 'Cause I Love Me So!

Materials: None.

Procedure: The children sing the following song. While singing, they touch the part of their body mentioned and act out the words of the song.

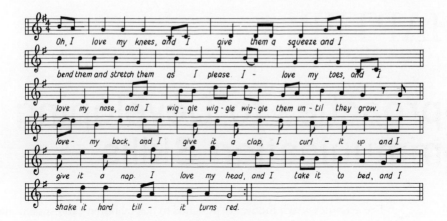

Oh, I love my knees, and I give them a squeeze,
And I bend them and stretch them as I please.
I love my toes, and I love my nose,
And I wiggle, wiggle, wiggle them until they grow.

I love my back, and I give it a clap,
I curl it up and I give it a nap.
I love my head, and I take it to bed,
And I shake it hard till it turns red.

Oh, I love my feet, because they're so neat,
And I kick them high till they fly in the street.
I love my shoulders, because they can shake,
Up and down, up and down and around the lake.

I love my hips and I take them on trips,
And I twirl them and swirl them with lots of dips.
Around and around and around I go,
And I hug myself, 'cause I love me so!

Variation: Each child finds a partner. While singing the song, she substitutes 'you' and 'your' for 'me' and 'my' and touches the appropriate part of her partner's body, ending with the two partners hugging each other!

Potential: A way to affirm one's body image, and that of others, that is sure to produce lots of laughter. It can be used as part of language work (developing vocabulary for different body parts), or within a Science topic on the human body.

CHAPTER 4

Approaches to Developing Communication Skills

The activities which follow are designed to help children express their ideas and feelings clearly, to focus their attention on whoever is speaking, to listen carefully, to reflect on what is being said, to observe the ways in which people communicate non-verbally, and to use their own bodies to communicate with others. It is worth noting that a number of the activities in chapter 3 are also effective in achieving aims related to communication skills. For example, **Interviews** (page 21) and **Police Officer, Have You Seen My Friend?** (page 25) involve both expressive and listening skills. **Feelings Walk** (page 23) requires a great deal of non-verbal communication. Similarly, some of the following activities, such as **Magic Microphone** (page 47), can be highly affirming experiences for children.

Activities focusing on communication skills need to be carried out with a particular awareness of the needs of children whose home language is different from the language used in school. Such children may need extra support during some of the exercises described below; difficulties they experience could be remarked upon in a negative way by English mother-tongue children, and this is extremely detrimental to the self-esteem of the child who is learning English. Children who are coping with the challenges of developing competence in two (or more) languages need to be actively protected from this sort of behaviour. Teachers must consciously avoid referring to them in class as 'non-English speakers', as this defines them only in terms of what they *cannot* do. Placing the emphasis on what they *can* do, i.e. that they can communicate very well in Hindi or Punjabi or Greek, conveys that their heritage and bilingual skills are valued.

Telephone

Materials: None. A large space is necessary in which all the children can sit in a circle.

Procedure: The first child in the circle whispers a brief message such as 'I'm your friend!' to the child on the right. That child passes the message to the next, and so on until it has gone all the way round the circle. The last person says the message out loud. The object is for the message to arrive without changes or distortions. When first introducing this game with young children, it is helpful to start with a very simple message, or even just one word, until the children can play with some success.

Variation: After some practice the group can try passing a simple message or word in another language, preferably one which is the mother-tongue of a member of the class. This could help English-mother-tongue speakers empathise with the challenges that children learning English face every day.

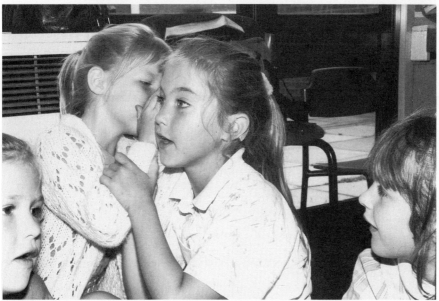

Playing **Telephone:** *Are you listening?*

37

Potential: A way to develop skills of listening and conveying messages. A discussion following the game can give rise to an awareness of factors that facilitate clear communication – such as careful articulation and good listening. Factors that impede communication, such as background noise or inattention can also be pointed out. Messages passed can be relevant to any sort of topic work; for example, if the class theme is houses, the message might be 'Do you live in a flat?'.

Source: Basic format first published in Prutzman et al (see Bibliography).

Notes of a reception class teacher on a session of playing **Telephone:**

'The original message sent had changed from 'I hope you'll be my friend' to 'Send the telephone' by the time it had gone all the way around the circle. We discussed why. A. said she hadn't been able to hear what B. had said, so she had simply changed it. That immediately brought out feelings of anger from several children toward those who deliberately change the message. I asked what they thought they should do if someone does that. There were several suggestions such as 'Don't let them play', and 'Make them sit at a table and watch.' C. finally said, 'You could just ask the person to say what they really heard'. The others agreed that this seemed a sensible solution.

Then D. (whose mother is French) said she had a problem because her father has been away on a trip and she's been speaking only French at home, and was having trouble speaking English in school – this provided a good opening for discussing the impact of language differences on clear communication.

At one point, E. said he had difficulty because he was sitting next to F., and she didn't speak English very well. I reminded him that F. speaks Italian very well, and that she is learning more English every day. I then asked the group what they could do to make this game easier for someone who is learning English. After thinking for a while, someone said, 'Do good listening.' I was glad that at least one English-mother-tongue child realised that communication is a two-way process, and that she had a responsibility to listen well. But I think that the effect of such games on the self-esteem of children who are learning English as a second language has to be carefully considered.'

Telegraph

Materials: None. A large space in which the children can sit in a circle.

Procedure: The game is played in the same manner as **Telephone,** except that a sequence of hand squeezes and pauses are passed instead of a verbal message.

Potential: A useful way to introduce the idea that not all messages are spoken ones, but that sometimes we communicate simply with our bodies. Used in the context of circle time, it helps focus attention and creates a feeling of group unity.

Source: Basic format first published in Prutzman et al (see Bibliography).

Human Chalkboards

Materials: Chalkboard and chalk.

Procedure: The children sit on the floor in a circle and turn towards the right, so that each child is facing someone's back. A child is chosen to draw with her finger a simple shape, letter of the alphabet or number, on the back of the person in front of her, the 'human chalkboard'. This tactile 'message' is passed around the circle and the last person draws it on the real chalkboard for the whole group to see.

Potential: Another way of looking at the concept of non-verbal messages. It also provides an alternative way of reinforcing letter recognition skills, or shape and numeral recognition when used as part of a Mathematics lesson.

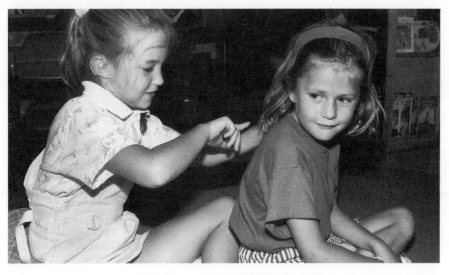

Developing non-verbal communication through **Human Chalkboards.**

Overloading

Materials: None.

Procedure: The children form groups of three, with one person sitting in the middle and one at either side. The children are given a topic to speak about, such as 'Things that make me feel angry'. At a signal from the teacher, the two children on the sides begin to speak about the topic simultaneously

39

to the person in the middle, who is instructed to pay careful attention to both. After one minute the children change roles; the exercise is repeated until everyone has had the experience of being in the middle. Feelings about the exercise can then be discussed.

Potential: 'Overloading' occurs frequently in the daily lives of young children. The exercise can help them to become more aware of this situation and the ways in which it impedes communication.

A group of seven-year-olds commenting on the exercise **Overloading:**
'I couldn't hear anything and it made me mad.'
'I felt bad because I couldn't understand both of them at the same time.'
'I wanted to tell them to talk one at a time.'
'We do this to Mrs B. (the class teacher) all the time!'

Cooper Says

Materials: None.

Procedure: This is a variation of the familiar 'Simon Says', where one child is chosen to lead the group through a series of motions, saying 'Cooper says do this.' The difference is that a child who does an action that Cooper did not say still remains in the game.

Potential: A simple activity which develops both listening and observation skills.

Source: Basic format first published in Prutzman et al (see Bibliography).

Farmyard

Materials: None. A hall or large open space in the classroom.

Procedure: The children stand in a circle and the teacher walks round to each one whispering the name of a farm animal in their ear. There should be approximately five or six children to each animal. Once each child has an animal, everyone closes their eyes and moves around the room, making their animal's sound. When two of the same animal meet each other, they hold hands and move round together, until everyone belonging to that group has found each other.

Variations: Very young children can select their animal by reaching into a box containing pictures of the animals, or better still, small plastic or wooden animal figures. Having a representation of their animal to hold during the game helps them to remember what sound they are supposed to be making. It is also recommended to discuss what sound each animal makes before beginning to play, and to practise each sound as a group. Nursery children can play the game with their eyes open.

Another variation would be to give the children names (or pictures) of household objects – running tap, boiling kettle, vacuum cleaner, typewriter, telephone – and ask them to group themselves according to the sounds those objects make.

Potential: This game requires children to listen carefully in order to find their group, and to co-operate by moving together as a group once they have found each other. It can be incorporated into a topic on animals, machines, etc., depending on the sounds children are asked to make.

A group of five-year-olds commenting on **Farmyard:**
'It was noisy!'
'It was silly!'
'I felt sad when I couldn't find my group, but then Lisa helped me.'
'It was fun all going 'moo!' at the same time!'

Pass the Sound

Materials: A space in which the children can sit in a circle.

Procedure: One child is chosen to make a sound which she passes to the child sitting next to her. The second child repeats it and passes it on, and in this way it gets passed to each person in turn. Once they are experienced with this procedure they can transform the sound into a new one as they pass it.

Potential: This game helps children develop the skills of focusing their attention and listening carefully, as well as building group feeling.

Source: Basic format first published in Prutzman et al (see Bibliography).

Listen and Clap

Materials: A favourite story-book.

Procedure: The teacher tells or reads a familiar story, and the children clap once (or raise their hands) each time they hear a chosen word which has been agreed on at the outset.

Variation: As their listening skills develop, the children can try clapping or raising their hands each time they hear the sound 'm' or 's', or any sound they are learning to identify.

Potential: A simple way of getting young children to focus on what they are listening to; children who are less able in terms of their listening skills are quickly drawn into participation by the enthusiasm of the rest of the group. The exercise can be used as part of a language lesson on initial consonant sounds, for example.

41

Escape from the Zoo

Materials: Small cards showing pictures of zoo animals or small plastic zoo animals of five or six different types, enough for one animal per child in the class (optional). Carpet squares or hoops, enough for one per child in the class (optional).

Procedure: The children sit on the floor in a circle (or on chairs, carpet squares or inside a hoop) and are each given the name of one zoo animal – younger children find it easier to remember their animal if they are holding a card with the animal's picture on it, or a small toy animal. The teacher, or one of the children, calls out the name of an animal. All the children holding that type of animal stand up, run around the circle and find an empty space to sit. Two or more animals at a time may be called. When 'Escape from the zoo!' is called, everyone gets up and finds a new place.

Variation: Children may be given cards of different colours; the game is played in the same manner, with everyone changing places when 'Rainbow!' is called. Similarly, the cards may show pictures of food, and all change places at the call of 'Market Basket!' The possible variations are unlimited.

Potential: An enjoyable game for very small children that builds a sense of group unity while encouraging the development of listening skills, and which can also be linked to vocabulary development on a variety of classroom topics (animals, colours, food, etc.).

For The Reading Corner

Would You Rather . . . by John Burningham (Jonathan Cape Ltd., 1978). Each page presents a new and more preposterous choice to make: Would you rather have a monkey to tickle, a pig to ride, or a goat to dance with? A delightful stimulus to discussion, and a useful way to develop the idea of similarities and differences within a group.

My Grandma the Monster by Ascher Davis (Women's Press, 1986). A young girl finds her grandmother a nuisance – until the day grandmother shares a story of playing monsters when she was young, and the two discover how much they have in common. A delightful story of inter-generational understanding, showing the ways in which relationships change when people communicate caringly.

How We Feel by Anita Harper and Christine Roche (Kestrel Books, 1979). With humorous pictures and a minimum of words, the book describes a range of feelings that children experience: belonging and being left out, being scared, shy, loved. A useful way of opening up discussion about feelings and the way that we express them. The illustrations show children from a range of ethnic groups.

Don't Forget the Bacon! by Pat Hutchins (The Bodley Head, 1976). A boy sets off to the market with a shopping list to remember, but on the way he gets it hopelessly muddled. Young children love listening for the mistakes as he repeats the list over and over – an enjoyable way to build listening skills.

The Surprise Party by Pat Hutchins (The Bodley Head, 1973). A rabbit gives a message to one of his friends, announcing that he is having a party. But as the message is passed from animal to animal it becomes increasingly garbled, with the result that no one turns up for the party. A humorous way of building an awareness of the importance of communication skills!

Purnima's Parrot by Feroza Mathieson (Magi Publications, 1988). Purnima desperately wants her pet parrot to talk, but all it does is squawk. Finally she realises that her parrot *is* talking – in its own language! A useful story for raising discussion about different languages and forms of communication.

A Fly Went By by Mike McClintock (Collins, 1961). A series of animals, each fleeing in fear from the one behind it, discover that the imagined danger was simply due to a misunderstanding. A classic humorous story of the problems that can arise from lack of communication.

On the Way Home by Jill Murphy (MacMillan, London, 1982). Claire scrapes her knee and sets off for home to tell Mum about it. On the way she meets a series of friends and explains her accident, with each version of the story (she was dragged off by a gorilla, nearly eaten by a giant, carried away by a flying saucer) becoming more far-fetched than the next. A story of fantasy and reality in communication.

'The Zax', in *The Sneetches and Other Stories* by Dr Seuss (Collins, 1961). Two stubborn creatures, a North-going Zax and a South-going Zax, find they are blocking each other's paths. They refuse to negotiate or compromise – to the inconvenience of the rest of the world. Useful for highlighting the need for listening to other's points of view.

Have You Seen My Duckling? by Nancy Tafuri (Puffin, 1984). A simple book with few words for very young children. Mother Duck has lost one of her ducklings, who is well hidden on each page. Observation skills are sharpened as children try to find each new hiding place.

Minute of Silence

Materials: None.

Procedure: Children sit or lie on the floor with their eyes closed, making no sounds for one minute. As children become accustomed to this practice, the time can be gradually extended. During this period they can be asked to listen for and recall sounds outside the room, inside the room or inside their own bodies; they can be directed to concentrate on their breathing and imagine they are breathing in and out through other parts of their bodies, such as the top of their heads or the bottoms of their feet. Simple guided imagery and visualisation can also be introduced (see **The 'Seed' Visualisation,** page 27).

Variations: Other relaxation/visualisation activities for use during the **Minute of Silence** may be found in Hendricks, G. and Wills, R., *The Centering Book,* and Hendricks, G. and Roberts, T.B., *The Second Centering Book* (see Bibliography, page 96).

Potential: This is a helpful practice, either at circle time, or at times of the day when children tend to get overly excited (just before lunch or after coming inside from the playground). It is calming and helps the children focus their attention and awareness.

> Comments from a group of six-year-olds on **Minute of Silence:**
> 'I could hear the wind blowing the leaves.'
> 'I heard some cars going by outside.'
> 'Was somebody snoring?'
> 'I could hear my heart going thump.'
> 'I thought about my Mum.'

Names in Motion

Materials: None.

Procedure: The class stands in a circle. One at a time a child goes to the centre of the circle and says her name, making a motion to go with the sound of her name, such as twirling around, stretching arms to the side and shaking the head, jumping and clapping on each syllable of her name – the possibilities are endless. When she finishes, the rest of the class repeats her name and motion in unison, while she stands in the centre. She then returns to her place, a new child comes to the centre, and the process is repeated.

Variation: Two children can come into the centre at the same time, hold hands, say their names – 'Samara and Jane' – and together make a motion that they have agreed upon, such as swaying from side to side. The class then repeats the names and motion. The game can also be played in silence, with the group repeating only the motions.

Potential: A way of helping children to remember and use each other's names, which is highly affirming since each child gets to be the centre of the group's attention. It can also be used to introduce the idea of non-verbal communication and the idea that our gestures and movements sometimes tell something about ourselves.

Use Your Senses

Materials: Blindfolds; a collection of objects to explore (this must be kept hidden); name badges with the words 'eye', 'ear', 'hand' and 'nose' (or picture symbols to represent these body parts).

Procedure: Children form groups of four, each wearing a different badge to represent one of the senses – sight, hearing, touch or smell (taste is omitted for safety reasons). Each child puts on a blindfold, except for the 'eye.' The 'eye' chooses an object for investigation by the rest of the group, using *only one sense*. She lets the ear listen to it, the hand touch it and the nose smell it. This must be done in silence. Once each child has explored the object, the eye asks them to tell each other what they heard, felt or smelt while remaining blindfolded. They then try to guess what the object was.

Potential: This activity develops the ability to communicate effectively within the group and to focus on what information is communicated to us through our senses. Children should have a chance to discuss how they felt about using only one sense, how important other group members were and which senses they tend to rely on more heavily. The exercise is especially effective when used after a nature walk, to identify objects, both natural and human-made, that have been collected.

> Comment by a teacher of six- and seven-year-olds on **Use Your Senses:**
>
> 'This really got them working together. The more unusual and less familiar the objects were, the better was the discussion and sharing. I particularly noticed M., who is quite difficult in the class. When he had a chance to be the 'eye', he seemed thrilled with the responsibility and took so much care over presenting the object to the others in the group.'

Going Dotty

Materials: Small coloured stickers, enough for one per child. There should be five or six different colours for a class of thirty.

Procedure: Children stand in a circle with their eyes closed. The teacher affixes a coloured sticker to the middle of each child's forehead. Once each

45

child has a dot, they open their eyes, and try to form groups of the same colour – without speaking.

Potential: Though it may take young children quite a while to figure out how to solve this problem, there is an enormous sense of satisfaction when they finally do. It is an enjoyable way of helping children to use non-verbal forms of communication and to respond to the cues given by others. It requires a high level of co-operation and shows that some tasks cannot be completed alone, but require the help of others. It is also a useful technique for getting children into mixed gender and ethnic groups prior to an activity which is to be carried out in small groups.

Source: Basic format first published in Pike and Selby (see Bibliography).

> Comments from a group of five-year-olds on **Going Dotty:**
> 'I couldn't tell what colour I was so I just put other people in their groups and then somebody put me in my group.'
> 'I helped three people.'
> 'I forgot to not talk.'
> 'Someone pointed me to the blue group so that's how I knew where to go.'

Co-operative Storytelling

Materials: A space in which all the children can sit in a circle. An interesting photograph or picture to stimulate ideas for a story.

Procedure: One person begins a story about the stimulus picture, saying a sentence or two. The next person adds another sentence or two and the story grows as it moves around the circle, until everyone has contributed.

Variations: It is often helpful to tape-record the story as it grows and play it back at the end. Children may also enjoy drawing pictures of the events in the story; these can be put together in sequence to form a 'Co-operative Storybook' with the words of the story written on the corresponding page. If the classroom has a listening centre, the recorded story- and picture-book can be placed there so that children can listen and read along.

Potential: This is an exercise that requires young children to listen carefully in order to create a coherent story as a group.

Source: Basic format first published in Prutzman et al (see Bibliography).

> **A co-operative story told by a group of five- and six-year-olds in a multi-ethnic school:**
> **A:** Once upon time, there was this little girl, and it was her birthday. So she decided to tell her mum that she wanted to go to the grocery store to get some balloons. So her mummy took her there,

and when she was walking she saw a little dog, and she petted it, and the dog bit her. And her finger was bleeding, and she went back home and put a plaster on, and it hurted her worse.

B: And when she was all better, her mummy let her go out again, but a cat scratched her.

C: Then her finger was bleeding again. Then she put another plaster on and she went out again. Then she got bit by a snake.

D: Then she was cry, because the dog hurt.

E: An animal came and bit the hand.

F: Then she told her mother that she wanted to go to the forest, and she saw a big crocodile, and the crocodile ate her. Then after that she thought she would take a little walk, but there was lots of people that were looking at her, and there was a little rabbit that liked her very much, and she thought she would take it for her birthday.

G: Her mother said, 'You can't take a rabbit at home.'

H: Then after that she saw a dragon and the dragon blew fire on her.

I: Then after the dragon just swallowed her, and the little baby rabbit. The baby rabbit liked the girl, and the baby rabbit had an idea. And the little rabbit said it to her. Then the girl made a big fire in his tummy, and the fire made the dragon sneeze, and he sneezed those two out!

J: After the dragon sneezed they fell into a river. It wasn't very deep. And the mummy thought she was dead.

K: And then she got swallowed up by a swordfish, and she got fire in its tummy, and she got out of there, and she ran into a snake thing, and the snake made her dead.

L: Her mummy give her something who was good for her, and she wasn't any more dead.

F: That's a good ending!

Magic Microphone

Materials: An old microphone from a tape recorder. Alternatively, a microphone may be improvised from card or scrap materials.

Procedure: The 'magic microphone' may be used during any group discussion as an aid to expression and listening. The teacher explains that only the person who is holding the microphone may speak; additionally, all the children must look at and listen to the person who is holding the microphone. When the speaker has finished, she hands it to the child next to her. Any child who does not wish to participate in the discussion may simply pass the microphone along.

Potential: Holding the microphone often helps draw out children who might be reluctant to speak; it is thus a good way of supporting second

47

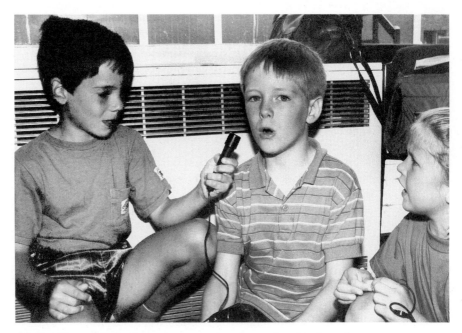

Magic Microphone: *Giving everyone a chance to speak and be listened to.*

language learners who may be left out or dominated in group discussions. The use of the microphone also helps more verbally assertive children listen and recognise that others have an equal right to express their opinions.

Bean Discussions

Materials: Two or three dried beans (or small pebbles, wooden inch cubes, small shells) for each member of the class; a jar or bowl.

Procedure: The children sit in a circle on the floor; each child is given an equal number of dried beans. The jar or bowl is placed in the centre of the circle. They are given a topic to discuss, such as 'What could we do to be helpful to the new child who will be joining our class tomorrow?' One at a time any child who wishes to speak may do so; as she finishes speaking, she places one bean in the jar. Once all her beans are in the jar, she has used up her turns to speak and must remain silent. Discussion continues until all the beans are in the jar or no one has anything else to say. Children do not *have* to use all their beans.

Potential: A helpful way of regulating a class discussion so that no one person can dominate, particularly useful in a class which includes children who are learning English as a second language. Holding an equal number of beans gives children a tangible symbol that they each have an equal right to participate in the discussion. An interesting technique to try during circle time, or for class discussions on any topic.

CHAPTER 5

Approaches to Promoting Co-operation

The activities in this chapter are designed to help children develop an awareness of other points of view; to be able to distinguish between problems which can be solved alone and those which require co-operation; to be able to modify rules through discussion and consensus; and to be able to work co-operatively with each other towards a common goal. The experiences are divided into two broad categories: active games or activities which require space for movement, and quieter board games and table activities that can be used in the classroom.

Active Co-operative Games and Learning Experiences

Musical Laps

Materials: One chair for each child in the group.

Procedure: The chairs are arranged in a circle facing outwards. The children walk around the chairs while the music plays and when it stops everyone must sit down. Each time the music stops, a chair is removed, but no players are eliminated. The children without chairs sit on someone's lap instead. At the end of the game, the entire class is sitting on one person's lap.

Potential: A variation of the traditional 'Musical Chairs', in which a player is eliminated with each round and the last child remaining is the winner. The adapted version builds a positive group feeling as no one is left out. The group has to co-operate to find ways for an ever-increasing number of children to sit on fewer and fewer laps – great fun! It is effective as part of a movement or PE session and makes a wonderful 'alternative' party game.

A teacher of five-year-olds played traditional 'Musical Chairs' with her class, followed immediately by a session of **Musical Laps.** She then recorded the discussion that followed (Note: Child D. in the transcript was the winner when the traditional 'Musical Chairs' was played.):

A:	I didn't like 'Musical Chairs' because I had to be out.
Teacher:	How did you feel about being out?
A:	Sad.
B:	I liked 'Musical Laps', because I like when we all fall down, and I like when A. sat on my lap.
C:	I liked it when everybody was all on one chair!
D:	I liked 'Musical Chairs' better, because I won.
Teacher:	D., if you hadn't been the winner, do you think you still would have liked it the best?
D:	Yes, because I like it and I had it at my party.
E:	Well, always when a person is the winner of something, they like it the best.
F:	I think if someone doesn't always win, they won't like it as much.
G:	I like 'Musical Laps' because nobody has to just sit and sit.
H:	It feels good to sit on someone else's lap!

Co-operative Musical Hugs

Materials: None.

Procedure: The children move freely around the room to any lively music. When the music stops, they find someone to hug. At the sound of the music, they continue moving as partners. With each pause, they join another group, until the entire class is hugging in one big group. Another way to play is for the teacher to call out a number each time the music stops, and the children must form groups of that size.

Variations: This can be played as a tag game, where children are only safe from the person chasing them when they are hugging another child.

Potential: This game helps children move together as a group, and also helps to ease any inhibitions about having positive physical contact with each other. By calling out the number to be included in each group hug, the teacher can also reinforce simple number concepts.

Source: Basic format first published in Orlick (see Bibliography).

Co-operative Musical Hoops

Materials: One hoop for each pair of children.

Procedure: Two children stand together inside a hoop, holding it at waist level, and begin moving around the room to music. When the music stops, they must join with another pair, putting their hoops together and all getting inside. They continue moving and joining together until the maximum number of children possible are inside the hoops.

Variation: Each child is given a hoop and finds a space in the room. The hoops are laid on the floor and the children stand inside them. When the music starts, the children move around the room skipping, walking, hopping or jumping. When the music stops, they must stand inside a hoop. With each pause in the music, the teacher takes away one hoop. The children must form groups of two, then three, inside the hoop, until the maximum number possible is reached.

Potential: Another way to encourage co-operation and fun without winners and losers, as well as helping children become comfortable with physical contact and developing counting skills.

Source: Basic format first published in Orlick (see Bibliography).

For the Reading Corner

Maxine's Piano by Chris Abuk (Longman, 1983). When Maxine and her family move to a new flat, they have difficulty getting their piano inside – until clever Maxine enlists the help of her friend the crane driver. A story of multi-ethnic co-operation, naturally and unpretentiously depicted.

Herbert and Harry by Pamela Allen (Hamish Hamilton, 1986). A tale of two brothers who live together happily until the day they discover a treasure in the sea. Herbert claims it as his own, makes off with it and then spends the rest of his life defending himself against people he imagines will try to steal it. Harry, meanwhile, grows old happily. A simply told story of the negative effects of greed and competition.

Dinosaurs and All That Rubbish by Michael Foreman (Puffin Books, 1974). After polluting the Earth, a man sets out to look for a far-away star to live on. While he is gone, the dinosaurs awaken from their sleep below the ground and restore the planet to its original green and blossoming state. When the man returns, the dinosaurs insist that everyone must share in caring for the planet. A fantasy, easily grasped by infant children, about collective responsibility for the health of the Earth.

It's Your Turn, Roger! by Susanna Gretz (The Bodley Head, 1985). When Roger the pig is told that it's his turn to set the table – again – he decides to go off to visit some other flats where, he is sure, he won't have to help. The visit to the neighbours makes Roger realise that helping with the chores isn't so bad after all – and that it's good to be home!

Helpers by Shirley Hughes (The Bodley Head, 1975). When Mum goes out for the day, Mick, Jenny and Baby Sue all help George, the babysitter, around the house. Can be used to develop discussion on the types of co-operation needed in running a home.

The Doorbell Rang by Pat Hutchins (The Bodley Head, 1986). Sam and Victoria are about to share a plate of biscuits – six each – when the doorbell rings. With two guests arriving, they realise they can still share the biscuits, but now there will be three each. The doorbell keeps ringing, guests keep arriving, and the children keep sharing – until the last surprise visitor arrives. A delightful story about co-operation, with mathematical applications.

Tom and Sam by Pat Hutchins (The Bodley Head, 1968). Tom and Sam are always competing with each other, until an embarrassing accident teaches them that they can live more happily by co-operating.

It's Mine! by Leo Lionni (Anderson Press, 1986). A fable about three quarrelling frogs, one who claims that the earth belongs to him, one who claims that the water belongs to him, and one who claims that the air belongs to her. A dangerous flood and a wise old toad teach them that sharing the island they live on brings them greater peace and happiness.

Swimmy by Leo Lionni (Abelard, 1975). A school of small fish discover that they can protect themselves from the dangers of the larger, fiercer fish by co-operating and swimming together as if they are one.

The Giant Jam Sandwich by John Vernon Lord (Jonathan Cape, 1978). When a village is threatened by a swarm of four million wasps, the villagers co-operate to trap them inside a giant jam sandwich. A humorous story, told in verse, of the way many people working together can accomplish what individuals cannot.

Crowns and Statues

Materials: One quoit per child in the class.

Procedure: Each child is given a 'crown' (a quoit) which they balance on top of their heads. (For older children, objects such as bean bags or small cushions may be used.) They then move around the room to music. If a quoit falls off, that child becomes a 'statue' and cannot move until another child comes along and replaces the quoit on top of the statue's head.

Variation: Very young children may have difficulty focusing on the task when there are large numbers of children moving around the room. It may be helpful to have the children work in pairs. One partner from each pair can sit in a circle around the sides of the room, while the other moves to music. If the moving partner's quoit falls off, she is frozen until the sitting partner comes and replaces it. The sitting partner then returns to her place. The partners should switch roles every few minutes.

Potential: A favourite during PE sessions, this game quickly conveys to young children the fact that they are interdependent and need to rely on each other.

Comment by a five-year-old on **Crowns and Statues:**
'I like when everyone was helping me to get not frozen, so I was trying to make my crown fall off all the time!'

Class Web

Materials: A large ball of string or wool.

Procedure: The children stand in a circle; one child takes a ball of wool, wraps it once around her waist, and passes it to someone else in the group. The process is repeated with each child until the whole class is joined together in a giant web. They can then disentangle the web by passing the yarn in the reverse order.

Variation 1: The game can be adapted by agreeing at the start on a 'rule' or reason for passing the yarn to a particular person. For example, the rule can be to pass it to 'someone you smiled at today'. This is a non-threatening choice, as by the time the game is finished, everyone is smiling at everyone else! Other possible rules might be used with children who know each other well, such as 'someone you played with today', 'someone you helped today', or 'someone you were kind to today'.

Variation 2: If there is adequate space, once everyone in the class is linked together by the wool, they can attempt to move as a group, keeping the shape of the web intact. With very young children this is best attempted in smaller groups at first. This process requires awareness of the group and the ways in which the movements of the individual will affect the shape of the whole web.

Potential: This activity provides a concrete experience of children's 'interconnectedness' in the class. Variation 1 should only be attempted with a group that has some experience of self-esteem and co-operative work; and 'rules' should be chosen that do not put children at risk of being left out. However, in a class which has consistently worked at building a positive sense of self-concept and group cohesiveness, children often seem to sense that the web is not complete unless everyone is included, and make an effort to involve each person.

This activity has been used by older infants to examine interdependence beyond the classroom as well. For example, a class that had been doing a

Linked together in a web of friendship.

study of a local park drew pictures of all the types of plants and animals they had found living there, as well as the soil and water, and pinned them on a display board. They then used pieces of wool to link 'things that need each other'. They linked green plants to both the soil and the water, as they realised that both were indispensible for life; they linked the insects to the green plants, as many types of insects eat leaves; they linked birds to the insects, which were their source of food. The final display made dramatically clear the complex interdependence which exists within food chains.

Source: Basic format first published in Orlick (see Bibliography).

A description of the **Class Web** activity by a teacher of six-year-olds:
'My class had taken the topic 'Our School' as a half-term's theme. We spent much of the time visiting persons who had important roles in the school – headteacher, secretary, cooks, dinner supervisors, caretaker, cleaners – seeing where they worked, talking about what they did, drawing their pictures, making a plan of the building and trying to locate the places where each member of the school community did their work.

One of our final activities was to use the **Class Web** idea, but to have each child take on the role of a person or group of people who were part of our school. They wore labels saying what their role was – teachers, parents, children, music teacher, as well as all the roles mentioned above. They then had to pass the ball of wool to someone in the circle who helped them, and to say how that person or group of people helped. It was fascinating to hear how their thinking developed, and how many layers of relationship they could grasp – the teachers helped the children learn to read, the children helped the teachers by tidying up, the parents helped the cooks by sending in the dinner money, the headteacher helped the dinner supervisors by paying them, the caretaker helped the music teacher by moving the piano, the secretary helped the parents by typing notices to go home – the children could have gone on all day. The web got so complicated to undo that I finally just took scissors and cut it!'

Co-operative Hot Potato

Materials: A ball or bean-bag.

Procedure: This version of the traditional game does not require the elimination of any players but allows all to be active and involved. The children sit in a circle and pass a hot potato (ball or bean-bag) until the caller shouts 'Hot Potato!' The person with the potato in her hands at this point moves out of the circle and joins the caller. The potato is passed again, but this time the two callers decide on a number, to which they count softly before shouting 'Hot potato!' together. As the game continues, more children join the callers, forming a new circle, until all children are in the callers' circle. The callers can agree either to decide together upon the number to which they will count, or let the last person to join choose the number.

Potential: The game builds a sense of group feeling by allowing everyone to participate throughout; it also builds counting skills.

Source: Basic format first published in Orlick (see Bibliography).

No Hands!

Materials: One small object – a ball, bean-bag or cushion – for each pair of children in the class.

Procedure: In pairs, the children move around the room to music, balancing the object between them. They can be encouraged to try balancing the object between different body parts: elbows, knees, backs, heads, feet.

Potential: This simple activity encourages children to work together co-operatively, to discuss how they might best solve the problem, and to use a good deal of creativity. It could be used during a topic on the human body to reinforce the vocabulary for the various parts.

Cars and Drivers

Materials: None. A hall or other fairly large open space is needed.

Procedure: The children find partners. In each pair, one person takes the role of the 'car' and the other the role of the 'driver'. The children are told

55

that the car must keep her eyes closed throughout the experience. She can begin by holding her hands just in front of her body, forming the car's bumpers. She can *only* move when and where the driver takes her. The driver stands behind the car with her eyes open and hands resting gently on the car's shoulders. The driver is responsible for guiding the car around the room and ensuring that no accidents with other cars occur. The driver may vary her speed, turn, stop, start again, or move in reverse. After about five minutes, the car and driver should switch roles.

After all the children have had a turn at each role, it is essential that they discuss their feelings about the activity. Was one role preferred to another? If so, which one? Why? How did it feel to co-operate? How did you communicate with each other? The discussion may reveal that some children enjoy the sense of responsibility/power of being a driver, while others feel hesitant about it. Some enjoy the role of the car and the sense of trust in the driver, while others may feel frightened and find it difficult to release control.

Variation 1: While the activity is best experienced in silence, some suggestions can help focus the attention of very young children. The teacher, or a child without a partner may call out, 'Red light', 'Green light', 'Winding road ahead', 'Icy patches – slow down'.

Variation 2: Trains: By linking in groups of three, the children can form a train. Everyone keeps their eyes open and the person at the head of the line (the driver) leads the train around the hall, avoiding collisions with other trains. Gradually trains can join up and form longer trains of six or nine children. To lead the train around safely requires an awareness of the group as a whole and the position of the last person in the line. The role of driver should rotate periodically.

Potential: As well as being an exercise in trust, co-operation and non-verbal communication, teachers have used it successfully in the context of a theme on transport to discuss speed, force, direction, etc.

> A five-year-old's comments on **Cars and Drivers** and **Trains:**
> 'I liked **Trains** better because you get to keep your eyes open. I liked it better because we were all connected together.'

Doggie, Doggie, Where's Your Bone?

Materials: A small object to use as a bone (a block of wood or a stiff piece of card).

Procedure: The class sits on the floor in a circle. One child is chosen to be the 'doggie' and goes out of the room. Another child is chosen to take the 'bone' and hide it by sitting on it or putting it in a pocket. The whole group then calls out 'Doggie, doggie, where's your bone? Someone has taken it from your home!' The 'dog' comes back inside, walks around the circle and tries to guess who has the bone. The other children try to help the 'dog' in the following manner: as she approaches the person with the bone, they clap their hands rapidly; if she moves away from the person with the bone, they clap more slowly, or stop as she moves to the opposite side of the circle.

Potential: This is an adaptation of a traditional game in which the 'dog' has three guesses, and the other children simply watch. The advantage of the adaptation is that it allows everyone to participate actively, and builds a positive feeling in the group by encouraging the children to help and support each other. Other simple guessing games can be adapted in the same manner, with the rest of the class helping the person who is guessing.

Shipwreck

Materials: None.

Procedure: One child is chosen to be the ship, and the rest are rocks. The 'rocks' sit on the floor, leaving ample space for a person to walk between them. 'Rocks' should not move about the room during the course of the game! The person who is the ship is blindfolded and must walk from one end of the room (the 'sea') to the other (the 'shore') without bumping into a rock. If she comes close to one of the other children, the 'rocks' must make the sound 'shhhh' (similar to the sound of waves on a rock) to warn her to change direction. When she reaches the 'shore', a new person is chosen to be the ship, and the original ship becomes a rock.

Variation: In addition to rocks, some children may be chosen to be sharks. If the ship approaches a shark, that person is responsible for giving one loud clap with her hands to warn the ship to change course. The children may devise other hazards and ways of warning the ship.

Potential: An enjoyable activity that encourages children to listen, help and become more aware of each other. It can also be used during a topic on transport.

Co-operative Pin the Tail on the Donkey

Materials: A blindfold; a large drawing showing an outline of a donkey; a tail cut out of paper or card; Blu-Tack® or drawing pins.

Procedure: The drawing of the donkey is hung on the wall. One child is chosen to begin, and is blindfolded. She is then given the tail and directed gently towards the drawing of the donkey. The object is to pin the tail to the correct part of the donkey. The children who are watching help to direct her by clapping rapidly when she is near the right spot (alternatively, they can say 'warm', 'warmer', 'hot' as she gets close, or give simple verbal directions, such as 'higher', 'lower', 'to the left', 'to the right'). Once the tail is pinned

57

on, the blindfold is removed so that the child can see the complete picture. Then another child may take a turn.

Variation: The different parts of the donkey can be cut out – head, neck, body, ears, tail, four legs, eyes – and given to various children. The child who has the body section can be blindfolded, and pins her piece to the drawing on the wall. Each child who follows her must add her piece, placing it in the correct position with the help of the children who are watching, until the entire animal is assembled. Other animals may be used, or a human figure, as well as objects which are fairly complex and made up of a number of parts (for example, a house may have pieces for windows, doors, roof and chimney).

Potential: A variation on a traditional game; this version eliminates winners and losers and reinforces the need to help each other in a humorous and enjoyable way. There is a positive group feeling when the task of completing the picture is finished. It also develops in the child who is blindfolded the ability to listen and follow directions. Depending on what image the children are assembling, it could be incorporated into a topic on animals, the human body, houses, etc. Concepts of spatial relations, as well as vocabulary, are reinforced during the process of playing.

> Comment by a reception class teacher on **Co-operative Pin the Tail on the Donkey:**
>
> 'I was surprised at how well they did it – they were really eager to help each other, which is the important thing. Some of the children who are learning English as a second language had difficulty at first, but they used the words 'yes' and 'no' to indicate when their partner was getting close to the right position. A few got overly enthusiastic and physically guided their friends!'

Lock and Key

Materials: A selection of 'lock' and 'key' shapes cut out of card in different patterns (see diagram below), enough so that each member of the group has one or the other.

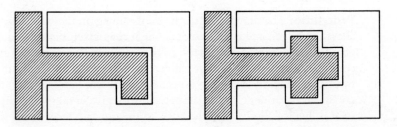

Procedure: Each child chooses one of the card shapes, either a lock or a key, and walks around the room trying to find a lock or key that fits together with hers.

Potential: An effective way to introduce the idea of interdependence and group work to very young children. It is also an enjoyable way of forming pairs for an exercise requiring partners. Visual discrimination skills are developed in completing the task.

Source: Graham Rowland, Feniton Primary School, Devon.

Picturematch

Materials: A set of assorted pictures cut into two parts. Pictures may be taken from magazines, or old greetings cards can be used.

Procedure: Children each receive one half of a picture; they then walk around the room, looking at each other's pieces, until they meet up with the person who has the piece which completes their picture.

Variation 1: Pictures can be cut into three or four pieces, depending on the age of the children.

Variation 2: Older children can be asked to look at their picture piece carefully for a minute. Then, keeping their pieces hidden against their bodies, they move around the room. As they meet another child, each tells the other as much detail about their piece as they can remember. When they think they have met someone whose picture piece completes theirs, they bring their pieces to the teacher, who lets them know if they are correct.

Variation 3: Pictures of women or men, girls or boys, in non-gender-stereotypical roles – for example, photos from the *Doing Things* pack, (see Bibliography, page 97) – can be cut in two, so that one piece shows the action being performed, and the other piece shows the person who is performing it. Children move around the room to find the person who completes their picture.

Potential: A simple co-operative activity which is satisfying when completed. Variation 2 requires the children to use observation, memory, listening and oral descriptive skills. Variation 3 will often provoke surprised comments such as '*Daddies* don't iron!' or 'Why is a *girl* using a punch bag?' These comments can form a useful springboard for discussing and challenging assumptions about gender roles.

Pictures can be selected on any theme, making this a particularly versatile activity that can be used with a range of classroom topics.

Source: Graham Rowland, Feniton Primary School, Devon.

Co-operation at the Art Table

Art activities provide abundant opportunities for co-operative work. Almost any art activity that can be done by individuals can also be done

59

co-operatively by groups. For example, young children often love to paint together at an easel, to fingerpaint together on one piece of paper, to use objects to print with to form one large design, or to make group collages. Especially with nursery children, the amount of discussion about what they are actually doing tends to be limited, and the work often develops without any particular plan, but the sense of having contributed to a pair or group project is reinforced. Slightly older children should be encouraged to actually negotiate together how they will go about working. The introduction of co-operative art activities should be balanced with a recognition of the need young children have to work on their own and explore the potential of various art media and techniques, as well as their own individual process of creation – vital to a sense of self-esteem.

Many excellent ideas for co-operative group art projects are to be found in *The Friendly Classroom for a Small Planet* by P. Prutzman, et. al., and *Art Therapy for Groups: A Handbook of Themes, Games, and Exercises* by M. Liebmann (see Bibliography, page 97).

Co-operative Board Games

Board games are increasingly used in schools to help teach and reinforce mathematical and language concepts with children under seven. Generally these are competitive games, which are often enjoyable for the child who wins, but may prove discouraging to the other players, particularly those who are less able. Following are descriptions of co-operative board games which have proved successful with children between the ages of three and seven. These are included in the hope that they will stimulate a re-thinking of the assumption that games must be competitive, and that they will encourage teachers to develop co-operative games and teaching materials for their own classes.

The Magic Tree

For 4–6 players, ages 3–4.

Materials:
A game board showing a path leading to a large tree (see illustration; actual size approx. 45 cm × 65 cm).
An assortment of fruit shapes to place on the tree.
A tortoise playing piece.
A dice.

Introducing the Game: It is helpful to read or tell the story *Tortoise's Dream* by Joanna Troughton (Blackie, 1980) first. This is a traditional story of the Bantu people told in a variety of African countries. It tells of Tortoise's dream of a tree upon which grow all the fruits of the earth. Many animals try to find it, but only Tortoise succeeds. If the book is not available, the game can still be enjoyed if the children are simply told that they are going to help Tortoise get to a magic tree full of good things to eat.

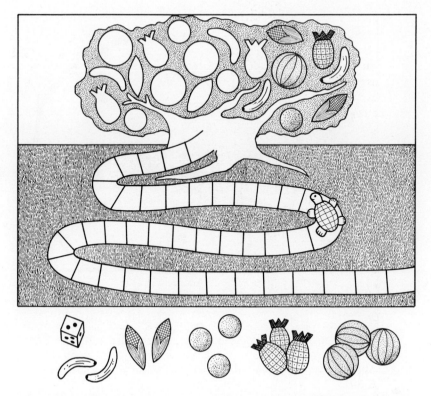

Procedure: The children take turns rolling the dice and advancing Tortoise along the path towards the tree. After each move they may also select a piece of fruit to hang on the tree, by matching one of the card shapes to the identical outline on the tree. Any fruits which are still missing when Tortoise reaches the tree can be distributed equally among the players, who can find places for them on the tree. (The fruit shapes may also be kept in a bag and children can draw them out at random to add more interest.)

Potential: The game helps to develop basic counting skills and one-to-one correspondence, while giving very young children a simple experience of working together to achieve a common goal. Many competitive board games for young children can be adapted in a similar fashion by having one communal playing piece, rather than one for each individual. The game also develops visual discrimination and matching skills; many traditional lotto games can be made more co-operative by having children work together to assemble one large picture as in **The Magic Tree** game.

Little Boy Blue

For 4 players, ages 3–4.

Materials:
A board which shows Little Boy Blue asleep and a fenced enclosure (see illustration; actual size approx. 45 cm × 65 cm).

61

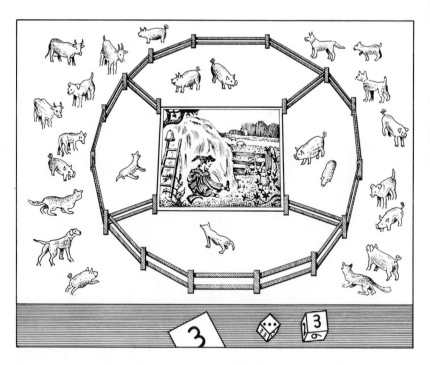

Approximately 40 small plastic animals (ideally, of four different types). A dice.

Introducing the Game: The children help prepare the board by placing all the plastic farm animals inside the fence. They then say the nursery rhyme as a group, and discuss what happened when Little Boy Blue fell asleep. They usually say that all the animals jumped over the fence. The children then take all the animals and place them outside the fence. The teacher explains that there are too many animals for Little Boy Blue to catch all by himself, so the children are going to help him get them back.

Procedure: The children take turns rolling the dice to determine how many animals to put back. (A dice with numerals can be used with children who need practice recognising numerals, or one with the traditional arrangement of spots can be used with those who need practice in counting.) A child who rolls a 3, for example, puts three animals back inside the fence. Animals may be taken from any part of the board and placed anywhere inside. It is important to emphasise this, as some children may feel that certain animals, or parts of the board, 'belong' to them. The game is finished when all the animals are returned.

Potential: The game provides another simple experience of working together to achieve a common goal. Knowledge of the nursery rhyme is not required for this game, since children who have never heard the rhyme enjoy counting and moving the animals none the less.

62   If four types of animals (chickens, sheep, cows and horses) are used,

children may decide to sort the animals as they return them, putting all of one type in one of the four sections of the fence.

> A five-year-old's description of the **'Little Boy Blue'** game:
> 'He (Little Boy Blue) went to sleep and all the animals got out. And then he went to sleep again. And then we got all the animals in, and when he woke up, he was happy. And he said, 'Thank you!'

The Bridge Across

For 4–6 players, ages 3–5.

Materials:
A 'Bridge Across' game board, showing a river and a house on either side (see illustration; actual size approx. 50 cm × 70 cm).
80 wooden cubes (2 cm square).
A dice.

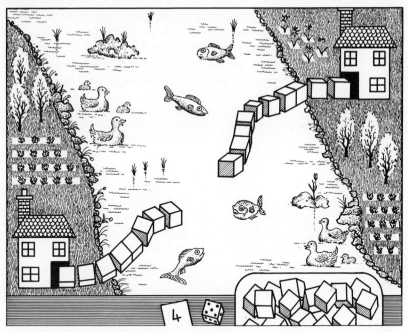

Introducing the Game: A helpful introduction to this game is to read or tell the story *The Bridge Across* by Max Bolliger (Andersen Press, 1980). This is the story of two quarrelling families living on opposite banks of a river. A friendship which develops secretly between their children causes them to reconcile their differences and they build a bridge across the river ending their isolation. Despite its unfortunately stereotypical portrayal of gender roles, it is a story of communication and co-operation which can be easily grasped by children under the age of seven.

63

If the book is not available, the children can be divided into groups of two or three sitting on opposite sides of the board and asked to imagine that they are two families living on different sides of the river. As they have no neighbours on their own side of the river and they are feeling rather lonely, they decide to build a bridge.

Procedure: The children take it in turns to roll the dice, first a child on one side of the river, and then a child on the opposite side. The number on the dice tells how many cubes the player may take to build with. They should begin building from the door of each house. The children all win when the two halves of the bridge meet in the middle of the river.

While adults or older children will see the task as placing the cubes in a diagonal line across the river, children between the ages of three and five do not yet have well-developed spatial concepts, and will often build in a variety of directions, without relating to what the others are doing. If this happens, it is best not to intervene immediately, but to wait and see if the children can work out for themselves the solution to the problem. If they continue building without reference to each other, the teacher can ask, 'Are the two sides of the bridge going to touch soon?', or 'What do we have to do to make the two sides meet?' This may prompt a child to try to change the direction of the bridge, sometimes to the objections of other players. Such an occurrence should be used as an opportunity to encourage discussion and decision by consensus as to how the task might be completed.

Variation: Older children might try to build the bridge using Lego®, rather then cubes. This would require visualising the structure in three dimensions, rather than as a simple line.

Potential: The game requires young children to all contribute to a common goal, and when the two halves of the bridge meet, the fact that they have succeeded by working together is immediately apparent to all. The game also requires the players to count with one-to-one correspondence, be aware of spatial relations, anticipate the outcome of their actions and communicate with each other about how best to build the bridge.

A teacher of four-year-olds commenting on **The Bridge Across** game:

'They loved it, and it was great because they could play it on their own without adult supervision. There was no fussing over the dice, or whose turn it was, and they could invent their own rules. The children went beyond co-operating just to build the bridge. They also independently developed a system of 'division of labour' within the families on either side of the river, with one child in charge of rolling the dice and telling the number, and the other taking responsibility for the actual placement of the blocks.'

Building a House

For up to 6 players, ages 5–7.

Materials:

A 'Building a House' game board with an outline of a house (see illustration; actual size approx. 45 cm × 65 cm).

6 envelopes (one per player) containing an assortment of yellow 'bricks' made of card (2 each of the following shapes: large rectangle, small rectangle, long thin rectangle, square, triangle).

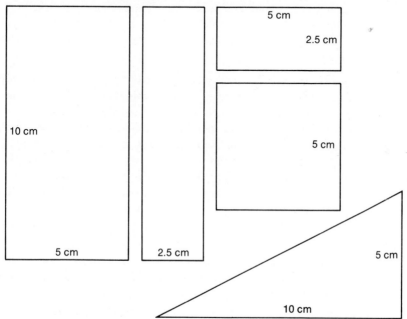

65

Each envelope should also contain one orange roof tile; suggested shapes are as follows.

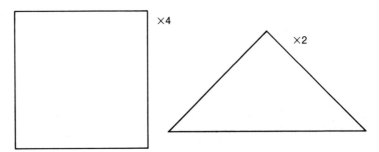

Introducing the Game: The players are told that they are going to work together to build a house using bricks. It is often helpful to ask such questions as:

Has anyone ever watched a house being built?
How many builders were working on it?
Is building a house something that one person can do alone, or do people have to work together to finish it?

This will help children to comprehend the idea that co-operation is necessary for many large jobs, and that in this game they will have to work together rather than compete with each other.

The children are told that they will each receive an envelope containing yellow bricks. There will also be an orange shape in the envelope, but this is to be used for the roof. They are reminded that before they can work on the roof, they need to build the walls of the house; they can be asked to explain why this is so. With younger children, it is helpful to first demonstrate the building process by laying down one or two yellow bricks at the bottom of the house.

Procedure: Each player is given an envelope full of bricks. Play proceeds with each child in turn placing a brick within the house outline (Blu-Tack® may be used to fix them in place). They should be careful not to cover the door or windows; if a child does this, she can be asked what the effect might be on the people who will live in the house. Any shape may be used, and if they are aligned correctly, they will fit like jigsaw pieces into the outline.

When the walls are complete, some yellow bricks will be left over. The children can now work on the roof. Each should have one orange shape, and all of the orange shapes are necessary to complete the roof, so they will have to work together and negotiate in order to arrive at a satisfactory arrangement.

Potential: This game develops children's awareness of spatial relations and basic geometric shapes. It also stimulates them to work together co-operatively, since their choice of which bricks to use will often be determined by the shape used by the preceding player.

Sometimes children will place bricks at an odd angle, making further building difficult. If this happens, it is best not to point it out, but to let the children discover for themselves what the problem is. A player who feels the position of a brick should be changed must first explain to the others her reason for wanting to do so; this type of discussion will develop negotiation skills, as well as extending vocabulary for expressing shape and position concepts.

With three- to five-year-olds, the game is more successful if the number of different types of shapes is reduced; eliminating the triangle and the long narrow rectangle makes it easier for them to see how the bricks fit together.

Comments from a teacher of six-year-olds on the **Building a House** game:

'It's really excellent for developing logical thinking. I have some children who aren't drawn to doing puzzles or that type of activity, because those are solitary activities, and they are more socially-oriented children. But they got really involved in this game because it had a social aspect. It was also good for some of the girls who had tended not to get involved in things requiring building or spatial relations.'

The Park Game

For 6–8 players, ages 6–12.

Materials:

1 'Park' game board (see illustration; actual size approx. 50 cm × 70 cm).

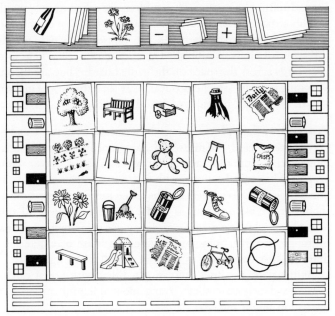

20 grey cards (10 cm × 10 cm) with pictures depicting various types of rubbish.

4–8 green cards (10 cm × 10 cm) with pictures depicting things one might find in an ideal park.

20 blank green cards (10 cm × 10 cm).
20 small cards with one symbol, either + or −.
Blu-Tack®.
Felt-tip pens.

Introducing the game: The children are asked to imagine that this is the neighbourhood in which they live; they are told that on this particular estate there is a large space between the houses in which people have been throwing all kinds of rubbish. The children can then help to distribute the grey cards across the space on the game board. They are then told that they are going to work together to clear away the rubbish and make the space into a park which can be enjoyed by all the people who live near by.

Procedure: Each player in turn draws a card from the + and − deck. If she draws a minus card, she must 'take away' one item of rubbish from the park. However, it cannot be merely 'thrown away'; the player removing it must suggest what will be done with it (re-use, repair or recycling are some possibilities). Other players may be asked for their suggestions and the group should arrive at consensus as to the fate of each piece of rubbish.

A player who draws a plus card may add something to the park using one of the green cards. Some of the green cards are blank, allowing players to draw in their own ideas as to what should be in this space.

As the park becomes increasingly filled with green cards, players can discuss and negotiate their arrangement. Helpful questions to guide the discussion might include:

Who do you think will want to use this space? Children?
Of what ages? Girls? Boys? Adults? The elderly?
Will everyone want to use the space in the same way?
Should the needs of some people have priority over the needs of others?
Why or why not?
Are there some items or areas that should be near each other? Are there
some that should be kept apart? Why?

Variation: Rather than create a park, the game can be structured to create a
wildlife garden, requiring the children to include all the plants and animals
that would make up the food chain.

Potential: This game requires a high degree of co-operation, developing
language, discussion and negotiation skills. It also encourages children to
explore the points of view of others by anticipating the needs and wants of
various groups in relation to the creation of the park.

The game develops certain concepts which are central to environmental
education, concerning management of resources and waste. Clearly, the
game will be most effective if the children have had some background in
environmental education, or if it is used in conjunction with a project on this
subject. However, even if children are unfamiliar with, for example, ideas
such as recycling or composting, they will derive considerable learning from
discussing the issues related to what will go into the park.

Some comments on the use of co-operative board games:

'The problem with these games is that they're too 'adult intensive'.
You have to have someone with the children all the time, and that ties
up one adult and we just don't have that kind of staffing. I did wonder
about using parent volunteers or one of the older junior children to
help.'

A teacher of five- to six-year-olds.

'I found I could leave a group completely on their own with these
games and that they could play happily with no conflicts requiring a
teacher's intervention. The children were so eager to help each other,
and spontaneously thanked each other when they did. They were still
discussing ideas that came up during the games for days after they had
been passed on to another class.'

Another teacher of five- to six-year-olds.

'I find these games very interesting because all the children are very
active. They discuss and negotiate frequently. No child felt hurt
during the games, so they will all return happily to do them. I
appreciate these games above all for the atmosphere of collaboration
they create, to know that to succeed at something one always needs
others, and the pleasure of sharing a collective success!'

A teacher of six- to seven-year-olds.

69

More Co-operative Board Games

Helping Hands and **Haunted House** are two more co-operative board games being produced by Philip & Tacey (see Classroom Resources, page 97).

In **Helping Hands,** players climb to the top of a mountain along a path of stepping stones. Whenever a player gets stuck in a hazardous spot, the others must co-operate to find the correct number of helping hands to pull her out. Everyone wins when the top of the mountain is reached and a picnic is shared by all! In addition to developing co-operative skills, the game gives plenty of practice with number bonds.

Inside the **Haunted House,** children must make their way through obstacles such as winding stairways and locked doors, and find a way to help each other so that everyone can escape! The key to getting past the obstacles lies in recognising initial consonant sounds. A fun-filled way to develop language and discussion skills, while learning to work together co-operatively.

Co-operative Squares

This is a well-tried exercise which helps participants to examine their own ways of reacting to a situation which requires collaboration to complete a task. It is most effectively done with upper primary and secondary students, or adults. This is the original exercise; it has inspired several variations which are more appropriate for children under seven, and these are also explained.

Materials: Five squares of card or paper, cut up according to the diagram below, for each group of five participants. All pieces marked A should be placed in one envelope, those marked B in a second, etc.

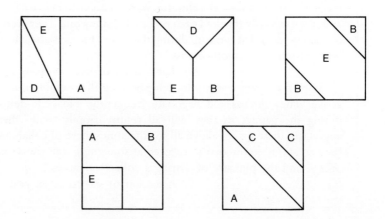

Procedure: Each person in a group of five is given an envelope. The group is told to make five squares, all of equal size. There are only two rules to be followed:

- Group members must not communicate, either verbally or non-verbally, while making the squares
- Group members are not allowed to give shapes to, or take shapes from, anyone else. They are permitted to place any of their pieces in the middle of the table, and to take pieces from the middle if they wish to do so.

Potential: Once participants realise that co-operation, rather than competition, is necessary in order to complete the task, a solution is usually found fairly quickly. The exercise can be used to stimulate discussion about co-operation and competition: How did those who 'finished' quickly feel? How did those who had more difficulty feel? What triggered the realisation that the group was going to have to co-operate? In what ways did participants co-operate? Did 'leaders' emerge within the group?

Source: Basic format first published in NEA Journal, USA, October 1969.

A discussion between five-year-olds after trying for nearly 40 minutes to complete **Co-operative Squares:**

A:	I don't like it, it was too hard.
B:	I don't want to do it again.
C:	Are we going to do it again?
Teacher:	Not today, but maybe some other time.
C:	Then I want you to do it with *other* kids.
D:	I'm tired, because my feet haven't been stretched.

Modified Co-operative Squares

Materials: Five squares of card, cut up according to the diagram below, for each group of five participants; five whole squares of the same size, but in card of a contrasting colour, to be used as templates.

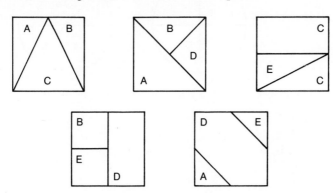

Pieces are placed according to their letter into one of five envelopes marked A–E. Each group of five children should be seated around a table.

Procedure: Each child receives an envelope. They are told that the aim is to use the pieces in their envelopes to make five squares of equal size. They may assemble their squares on the square templates. They may not take any shapes from each other, but can place shapes they do not need in the centre of the table and anyone may take pieces from the centre of the table. (It often helps to place a box in the centre to help children realise where to put their shapes.)

Children should discuss their feelings about the exercise immediately after completing it. They may express frustration, anger or possessiveness, as well as pride in completing the task and satisfaction at helping another or being helped. It is essential to get them to realise that this is a task that cannot be completed alone.

Potential: The fact that there is more than one possible solution in this variation makes it less frustrating for young children. Allowing them to talk helps them to reason aloud and to develop a problem-solving strategy. Provision of the whole squares is helpful for children who have not yet acquired the abstract concept of a 'square'. The exercise is most useful in the context of Mathematics work on shape.

Co-operative Circles

Materials: Five circles cut from card according to the pattern below (**a** is a half circle, **b** is 1/4 of a circle, **e** is 3/8 of a circle, **f** is 1/8 of a circle):

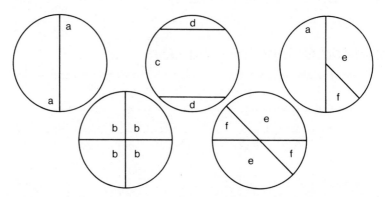

The pieces are sorted into five envelopes in the following manner:

1 **a, d, f**
2 **b, d, a**
3 **c, b, b, b**
4 **e, f, f**
5 **a, e, e.**

In addition, five whole circles should be cut from card of a contrasting colour for children to assemble their circles on.

Procedure: The game proceeds as for **Modified Co-operative Squares.**

Potential: Another way of introducing the idea of co-operation and developing shape concepts at the same time. The circle is the easiest geometric shape for young children to understand, and this activity is thus useful for children who may not yet understand what a square is.

A discussion by a group of four- and five-year-olds after playing **Co-operative Circles:**

A: It was hard!

B: It was easy, because C. gave me some pieces.

C: Well, when it looked like there weren't enough pieces, I had a piece that would fit into the puzzle. So I put it on.

Teacher: How did you feel about giving up one of your pieces?

C: It was easy, because I knew we could make two more out of them.

D: It was hard, because I didn't have enough pieces to make the circle.

E: Nobody did, so you had to give something away.

A: I thought if I give something away, I won't have enough pieces to do it.

C: But if you give them away, you can make the circle.

B: I felt angry when someone was keeping their pieces to themselves.

C: But when I saw someone had a piece I needed, I just asked them.

A: I didn't have enough pieces, but C. gave me some.

B: Yes, and E. gave me some. And then I felt happy because I made the circle.

E: You have to just, everybody give some!

Co-operative Faces

Materials: The four colour photographs of children (at the end of this book, following page 98) cut into pieces according to the suggested guidelines overleaf: three pieces per photo if they are to be used with three- to four-year-old children, five pieces per photo for five- to six-year-olds, and seven pieces per photo for children aged seven and older.

For 3–4-year-olds   For 5–6-year-olds   For 7+ year-olds

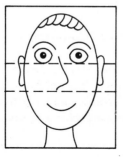 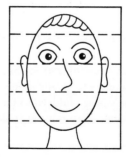 

The pieces should be mixed up and distributed equally among four envelopes.

Procedure: A group of four children is seated around a table. They are each given an envelope and told that the object of the game is to make four faces. The rules are the same as for **Modified Co-operative Squares,** as are the guidelines for debriefing.

Potential: Because the photos show children of different genders and ethnic groups, in the course of the exercise comments often arise about inter-group differences and similarities. The exercise provides a non-threatening context in which to discuss such potentially sensitive issues. The discussion might be guided by such questions as: How did you know this person was a girl/boy? How are the faces different? How are they similar? Are there more similarities or more differences? The exercise can be integrated into a topic on 'Myself', or into science work on the human body, or the diversity of living things.

As the human face is a more basic and recognisable unit than squares or circles, this exercise can be used with very young children.

CHAPTER 6

Looking Beyond the Activities

Children can begin developing the interpersonal skills and attitudes which form the foundations of global education from their first days in school. While their notions of global dynamics will obviously remain limited by their level of intellectual development, they can nonetheless start building respect for themselves and others, valuing diversity, identifying their own feelings and empathising with those of others, listening and expressing themselves effectively, negotiating, considering other points of view, co-operating and resolving conflicts peacefully.

As teachers experiment with the types of activities described in chapters 3–5, however, they often discover that there are larger implications to their work. These can be broadly grouped into two categories: implications for the individual classroom, and whole-school implications. An overview of these would include the points listed below.

Implications for the Individual Classroom

- Work on self-esteem, communication and co-operation will be most effective if begun early, in ways appropriate to the age-group.
- Activities in these areas need to be carried out on a consistent basis.
- The classroom atmosphere must be in harmony with the aims of the activities.
- Value must be given to the learning process as well as to the products of learning.
- Situations where children need disciplining can be used as part of the learning process.
- The physical organisation of the classroom can support the development of self-esteem, communication and co-operative skills.
- Children can be given responsibility for real decision-making in the classroom.
- The learning process can support children in taking meaningful, effective action in the outside world.

Implications for the Whole School

- Relationships between members of the teaching staff should ideally reflect an atmosphere of co-operation.
- A degree of devolution of authority may take place, so that there is an increased staff input into decision-making.

- Non-teaching staff can be recognised for the significant impact they have on children's lives.
- Parent education can become an important means of developing support for the aims of the school.
- In-service training is vital to the implementation of a whole-school approach to global education.

Let us look at each of these points in more depth.

Classroom Implications

Work on self-esteem, communication and co-operation will be most effective if begun early, in ways appropriate to the age-group.

Teachers who work in the field of global education suggest that the nursery and infant years may be an optimal time for the development of such interpersonal skills; if such work is left for the junior years, teachers may be faced with the task of finding ways to help children 'un-learn' negative habits in their ways of relating to each other.

Consider, for example, the observations of two different teachers on their children's co-operation skills. The first is from a teacher of seven- to eight-year-olds who tried the **Building a House** game (page 65) with her class:

> '. . . There were some problems. When I stayed next to the children, the game went well. But when I left, there were tensions. Why? The children are still, at this age, very egocentric and they have a very strong sense of competition (without the idea of fair play!). A game where nobody wins, but where everyone collaborates, was an idea a bit difficult to internalise for them.'

The second is from a teacher of four-and-a-half-year-olds who introduced a commercially produced competitive game, 'Eensy Weensy Spider' (Orchard Toys, 1976), to her class. The object was to roll the dice and move a toy spider up a 'water spout'; the first child to reach the top would be the winner.

> 'The children quickly caught on to the idea of rolling the dice and counting with one-to-one correspondence. As they progressed up the water spout, A. remarked, 'I'm almost there.' On the next roll of the dice, B. reached the top. He said with delight, 'That was fun. I'm going to go down and start all over again!' He moved his spider to the starting position, and continued taking his turn rolling the dice; as the other children reached the top, they all did the same. Their play went on for more than a half hour; no one ever remarked about who was 'winning'.'

These children were playing for the sheer joy of playing, as is natural for children in the early childhood years who have not been trained to do otherwise. They spontaneously transformed a competitive game into one that, if not co-operative, at least did not involve winning and losing. By contrast, the children who were three years older were having difficulty playing a co-operative game because they could not release their ingrained notion that games must be competitive. Teachers who work with older primary school children or adolescents may face the difficult task of undoing damage done by years of emphasis on competition. Nursery and infant teachers are fortunate in that they need do very little 're-training' of children in order to encourage them to think co-operatively; such behaviour is in fact a fairly natural occurrence among young children.

Activities in these areas need to be carried out on a consistent basis.

If used only sporadically, the activities described in chapters 3–5 are unlikely to promote deep and lasting changes in the way children feel about themselves and others. If the activities are seen merely as an occasional pleasant break from routine, children will quickly absorb the unspoken message that the development of personal and social skills does not really have a high priority in school. They will, in addition, be less likely to give fully of themselves, sharing their thoughts and feelings, if they sense that such information is not truly valued. If implemented on a regular basis, work involving affirmation, communication and co-operation can build a climate of trust between the children themselves, and between the children and the teacher. Such a climate of trust, in which each child feels personally valued, facilitates the expression of the emotions and of varied points of view. The teacher must be aware that these may sometimes include racist or sexist points of view. Once these are expressed they can be dealt with directly, providing that care is taken to protect the feelings of any child who may be the target of such comments. In classrooms where such attitudes never come out into the open and thus are not challenged by teachers, the assumption is made that 'We don't have that problem here, the children never bring it up'; the opportunity to make a positive intervention is lost.

The classroom atmosphere must be in harmony with the aims of the activities.

As teachers work with the approaches described on page 75, a shift is often made from seeing the beginnings of global education simply in terms of a collection of activities, to recognising that it involves changes in attitudes that will infuse the whole atmosphere and value system of the classroom. Can self-esteem effectively develop in a classroom in which a child spends a morning working on a page for an affirmation notebook, and is then criticised for being slow as she struggles to master the complexities of tying her shoelaces? Are children likely to miss the underlying message conveyed by a teacher who spends the first fifteen minutes of the morning playing a game that develops their listening and expressive skills, and for the rest of the day expects them to get on with their work in silence? Is it not possible that children who are encouraged to co-operate during active games in the hall might wonder why they are reprimanded for later trying to help a friend with a Mathematics problem? A large part of the development of self-esteem, communication skills and co-operation goes on not only during effectively-planned experiences of the type described in the earlier chapters, but in the multitude of teacher–child and child–child interactions that occur each day. It is thus vital that the medium of the classroom climate is in harmony with the message conveyed by such activities.

Value must be given to the learning process as well as to the products of learning.

Children can be given recognition for all that is positive in their efforts and intentions (whether in artistic creation, mastering a new physical skill, completing an academic task or working through a challenging social situation), even if the outcome is not quite what the teacher anticipated. Attention should be given to the *processes* by which the children solve problems, not only to whether the outcome or product was successful in the teacher's eyes.

Imagine a situation that might typically arise in a classroom: a child comes to the teacher proudly displaying a Lego® model she has just finished, saying 'It's a boat!' An almost reflexive response on the part of the teacher who has the child's self-esteem in mind, might be to smile and say, 'Well done!' or 'Isn't that lovely!', comments which can be considered affirming. The teacher could, however, have reacted in the following way:

> 'So you've made a boat – tell me about it . . . What does this part on top do? . . . How did you manage to attach it? . . . Did it take long to make? . . . Have you finished working on it or are you going to add anything else to it? . . . How did you feel when you were making it? . . . What do you think would happen if you actually put it in water? . . . If you could really sail on it, where would you go? . . .'

Notice that in the second example, the teacher uses no adjectives! Rather than make a judgemental statement about the quality of the child's product, the teacher encourages her to reflect on her own process of making the boat, giving room for the child to express her own satisfaction or dissatisfaction. The open-ended questioning can extend language, discussion, imagination and experimentation. Clearly, no teacher will have time to engage every child in a conversation of such length about every piece of work produced during the course of the school day. Yet it is worth bearing in mind that time spent listening with *genuine* attention and interest to a child probably has more potential impact in terms of fostering self-esteem than superficial compliments do. When an adult gives of her time and energy in this way, the unspoken message conveyed to the child is 'You are a person worth spending time with and I enjoy being with you!'

Situations where children need disciplining can be used as part of the learning process.

Occasionally teachers have reported the feeling that supporting children's self-esteem is incompatible with maintaining discipline; as one teacher asked during an in-service training session, 'If we can't do anything to harm their self-concepts, then how can we ever tell them off?' Such a question reveals that the discipline process is being seen as essentially punitive; the process can, however, also be viewed as essentially educative.

When exploring the effects which different approaches to discipline have on self-concept, it is helpful to make a distinction between disapproval of a specific behaviour and disapproval of the child who has performed that behaviour. The language used by teachers in discipline situations often contains negative messages or underlying assumptions (conveyed with varying degrees of explicitness) such as, 'You are stupid', 'You are bad', 'You are clumsy', or 'You will never change'. Aside from hurting children's feelings, teachers would do well to consider whether expressing such attitudes constitutes effective discipline. Research has produced abundant evidence, dating from the 1960s, to show that teacher expectations strongly influence children's performance in both academic and social areas (1). If teachers create a classroom climate in which naughty, stupid, careless behaviour is expected, they should not be surprised to find that such behaviour is exactly what will ensue.

No child is intrinsically bad or unworthy; however, some actions are inappropriate or unacceptable in the classroom, and the language used to communicate that point of view does matter. Compare, for example, some possible teacher responses to a child who has hit another during an argument at the sand tray:

> 'What's the matter with you? Stop being such a bully!'
> 'Every time you play in the sand you end up fighting. Come away from there right now.'
> 'Hitting can hurt someone and I can't let you do that.'
> 'What is the problem here? How are you feeling right now? Can you tell her with words what it is that you want? How do you think she is feeling right now?'

The first two comments express a belief that aggressive behaviour is characteristic of the child. The third comment expresses firm disapproval of the action of hitting, but does not assign negative characteristics to the child. The final response goes further by encouraging the child to put into words what the problem is, so that the children begin to learn how to handle conflict without physical aggression and to understand the effects of their actions on others.

Children in conflict need to begin by defining exactly what the problem is. It is not uncommon for young children to have a complete misunderstanding of each other's feelings, and expressive and listening skills can be usefully employed to clarify both perspectives. Once the nature of the problem is clear, the children can be encouraged to suggest possible solutions; onlookers may be brought in to assist in case of an impasse. The children can also be encouraged to anticipate the possible outcome of such solutions: How will that make *you* feel? How will that make *her* feel? What do you think might happen next? Though simple, such questions pave the way for the type of 'future' thinking that will be a feature of later work in

79

global education, as well as encouraging children to develop an awareness of another's perspective. As the following example from a nursery teacher shows, even young children can be helped to use this sort of reasoning in a situation where there is conflict:

> Two four-year-olds were playing on a large tyre embedded in the ground. One of the boys was sitting on the tyre and the other was pulling at him and saying, 'I want a turn'. As the boy on the tyre was in danger of being pulled off, I intervened:
>
> Teacher: Michael, can you tell me what the problem is?
> Michael: Craig won't let me have a turn on the tyre.
> Teacher: Craig, can you tell me about it?
> Craig: Well, I was on first and he keeps pulling me off.
> Teacher: Is that right, Michael?
> Michael: Yes, but he won't let me play.
> Teacher: Michael, what might happen if you pulled Craig off?
> Michael: He might bump his head.
> Craig: And it would hurt.
> Teacher: Is there any way you could both get to play on the tyre?
> Craig: Well, I had it first.
> Michael: I can come on too, at the same time.
>
> Craig does not look too happy at first, but then Michael slides down the edge of the tyre on to the ground, falling on his bottom. They laugh and appear happy at this solution, both climbing on and sliding off together.

Such reasoning with children about the motives for their own behaviour, the possible motives of others and alternative ways of behaving, has been found to increase children's ability to take the point of view of another and to empathise (2). Consensus on a solution may be slow to arrive, but if the temptation to impose a solution can be resisted, the children will gain important experience in taking responsibility for their own actions and feelings. The implication of such an approach is that conflict in the classroom is not simply an annoyance which must be remedied by swift adult intervention, but it can be used as an opportunity to help children build the interpersonal skills necessary for good group relations. Mastering such interpersonal skills and developing greater self-reliance in dealing with conflict can be a highly affirming experience for young children.

Consider the following example of a teacher of five-year-olds who attempted to evaluate the effect of a year's work on affirmation, communication and co-operation on the conflict resolution skills of her class. This was done through the use of an interview and a survey of playground behaviour, carried out in the autumn and the summer terms, with both her class and a comparison group which had not received any special programme. She describes the results obtained overleaf. Though not a rigorously scientific evaluation, the results at least suggest a trend towards improved conflict resolution skills in the class studied and suggest that positive social behaviour can be encouraged through the use of the types of learning activities described in chapters 3–5.

Conflict and harmony: both can be learning experiences in the infant school.

81

'The first approach to evaluation that I tried involved showing photographs of typical conflict situations on the playground and asking the children what they thought they would do in such a situation. One result was that by the summer term, the children in my class were considerably better than the comparison group at describing what the children in the photos might be feeling. Both groups were proposing more co-operative solutions in the summer than in the autumn. But in my class, children were giving more reasoned answers – explaining the solutions in terms of how the parties involved might feel and what might happen next. In the comparison class, children tended to just say, 'They should share.' I had a feeling that they were telling me what they thought I wanted to hear; I felt more children in my class were telling me what they really thought. Perhaps an outcome of the work on self-esteem, communication and co-operation was a level of trust that allowed them to feel secure about expressing their own opinions.

In my class, a number of children proposed 'Tell a teacher' as a solution to the conflict in the autumn, but none did in the summer – perhaps they were developing the idea of taking more responsibility for their own conflicts; this seemed to be borne out by the playground survey as well.

What children say they will do in a conflict situation and what they actually do may be quite different! Because of this reservation I did a survey of behaviour on the playground in the autumn and summer (five days each term) for both classes, looking at how children actually solved conflicts over toys.

While the comparison class didn't particularly resort to telling a teacher when they had a problem, this was a predominant strategy among my class in the autumn; however, it diminished dramatically over the course of the year.

Sharing, or using a toy together, was the most commonly occurring co-operative solution. The number of incidents of sharing doubled over the year in the comparison class, and increased fivefold in my class!

When I added up the total number of conflicts which occurred each term, I found that the number increased over the year in the comparison class, and decreased in my class. In the comparison class, about one-third of the conflicts were solved co-operatively, in both autumn and summer. In my class, about one-quarter of the conflicts were solved co-operatively in the autumn, compared to two-thirds in the summer! A more carefully controlled study would have to be done in order to determine if this sort of work is really producing long-term effects, but it was exciting to be able to stand back from teaching and see tangible evidence of some of the kinds of changes I had felt were taking place in the children.'

The physical organisation of the classroom can support the development of self-esteem, communication and co-operative skills.

In examining the physical arrangement of the classroom, having tables or desks pushed together to form clusters is preferable to having desks in rows. Tables facilitate the use of small group and co-operative learning strategies, and convey to the children that interaction and collaboration is valued and sought after. A classroom arranged with learning centres, rather than focused on a teacher at the chalkboard at the front of the room also encourages small group work, and conveys to children that the teacher is not the sole source of

82

knowledge, but that they have a wealth of ideas and experiences to share with each other as well. Such classroom organisation can provide children with an element of choice and control over their daily activities. The opportunity to choose their own experiences helps children take responsibility and develop a clearer sense of their own abilities and interests. Classrooms for young children should provide adequate space for the entire class to sit together on the (preferably carpeted) floor for group discussions. The effectiveness of such discussions will be increased if the children can sit in a circle, with every member of the group being able to see everyone else – listening skills are much improved by this seemingly simple arrangement. Display boards and display areas offer an important means of communicating to the children that both they and their work are valued. Displays need not be elaborate in order to convey respect for children's work; indeed, overly elaborate displays may emphasise the teacher's efforts and detract attention from the children's creations.

Children can be given responsibility for real decision-making in the classroom.

By giving children the chance to participate in making decisions that affect them in the classroom, teachers can put into practice the principles of co-operative group living. Games and learning experiences of the type described in chapter 5 help children to learn the skills they will need for co-operation; having the chance to make real choices between alternatives, rather than relying on the teacher as the ultimate decision-making authority, provides the opportunity to learn *through* the process of co-operation itself. One approach to the process of democratising the classroom is to open decisions which are normally made by the teacher to discussion with the children:

What games shall we play at our party?
If we don't have space for both a woodworking bench and a sand table, which would we prefer to have in the class?
When we're ready to change the dramatic play area – shall we have a shop, a vet's or a hospital?

At times children will reach a clear consensus on such questions. At other times it may be feasible to have them vote and let the majority decide. Young children, if asked to vote by raising their hand for the option they prefer, will often raise their hands for several or all of the options, rendering decision-making impossible. The following technique can facilitate the voting process.

Each child is given a small box of uniform size (the type in which individual portions of fruit juices are packaged is ideal). These can be covered with coloured paper and decorated with a picture of the child to whom it belongs (photographs could be used). Each child's name should also be visible.

On a large piece of card the teacher should prepare a grid, as in the

83

diagram below. Each square on the grid should be the size of one of the children's boxes. The children are now ready to cast their votes by placing their boxes on this grid.

Suppose that a cooking project is planned for the next week. Some children want to make biscuits, while others want to make soup. The teacher draws a quick sketch of each of the options on two pieces of card and lays them at one end of the grid. One by one, the children place their boxes on the grid in line with the picture which shows their preference.

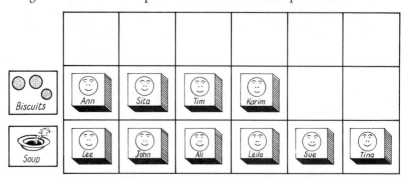

When this process has been completed, it will be clear to all which choice was preferred, and children will usually accept the decision of the group. In the event of a 'tie', each child can be asked to find a person who made a different choice and spend a minute or two explaining to each other why they chose the option they did. The voting process can then be repeated; some children may have changed their minds during the discussion. In addition to ensuring that each child only votes for one option, this method stimulates mathematical vocabulary, counting, and the skills of creating and reading simple graphs.

As children become experienced with this process, worthwhile questions for discussion can be raised, such as:

- Are there ever decisions which satisfy everyone?
- Are there ways to take into consideration minority viewpoints?
- What sorts of responses are appropriate for the minority that does not get its own way?
- Is doing what the majority wants always the fairest way?

Once the children become familiar with voting on simple questions like those listed above, they can use the same technique to begin to express their opinions on more complex issues: What should we do about children who throw sand? What can you do if someone calls you a name? What rules are important to have in the classroom?

Regardless of the level of complexity of the issue under discussion or what type of decision-making process is employed in the class, the fact that children's opinions are sought conveys to them the message that their teacher values and respects their ideas. Such an experience is deeply affirming. So too is seeing those ideas put into action; this is one of the most empowering experiences a child can have, and the sense that one's thoughts and feelings can make a difference in the real world is an essential component of the development of a global perspective.

Teachers of young children may need to reconsider their role if they wish to increase the children's level of responsibility and participation in the classroom. They may find that they gradually turn over some of their traditional power and authority to the children in ways appropriate to the age of the class. Despite the fact that children will at times choose courses of action that would not have been the teacher's preference, she must be prepared to abide by their decisions once she has indicated that their input is sought and valued. She will need to see herself less as someone who imparts knowledge, and more as one who facilitates the unfolding of her students' emotional, social and intellectual potential. She will at times find herself a participant in the learning process, rather than a director of it.

Such a shift in the teaching role may initially provoke a degree of internal conflict for the teacher. It will in all likelihood contrast sharply with the role she learned during her professional training, as well as with her own childhood experience of schooling. She may find herself examining long-held assumptions about the teaching and learning process, about the roots of motivation to learn and about the capabilities of children under seven. She is also likely to be rewarded with a deeper knowledge of the children as whole people; through the planning of learning experiences which draw on a range of human capacities simultaneously, she is apt to see positive outcomes in both the intellectual and emotional development of her students.

The learning process can support children in taking meaningful, effective action in the outside world.

Projects which involve taking real action in the school or local surroundings can help children to put communication and co-operation skills into practice, often with highly affirming consequences. One example is this recycling project undertaken by a reception class teacher:

'The recycling project started in a small way. The reception class children complained one day about the rubbish – crisp packets, aluminium foil, sweet wrappers – that was blowing into their playground from the older infants' play area. I asked the children during circle time what they thought they could do about this problem. They decided to collect all the rubbish into a large bin-liner. They did this the next day.

Things were fine for about a week; then a new accumulation of rubbish began finding its way onto the playground. Again I asked the children what they thought could be done. They decided to collect the rubbish again, but some children remarked that the older ones would just keep throwing their rubbish on the ground. I asked if there was any way to get them to stop doing that. The children decided to bring the rubbish they had collected to assembly and display it before the whole school, making a plea for the older children to use the rubbish bins provided. This was done, and some improvement followed, although the children found they still had to periodically collect rubbish that was dropped over the low playground fence by passers-by.

85

At this point, I read the class *Dinosaurs and All That Rubbish* by Michael Foreman (Hamish Hamilton, London, 1972). They particularly remarked on the illustrations of the polluted planet created by the humans, and the contrast with the clean and colourful environment created by the dinosaurs. I invited the children to try making pictures of their impressions of a clean and a polluted world. This culminated in two huge group collages being made, one full of rubbish and filth, the other showing a healthy environment in which plants and animals were thriving. The children dictated lengthy stories to accompany each, and they were hung in the reception class entrance.

I then introduced the concept of recycling. Several children already knew that some glass bottles could be returned to the shops and re-used, but none were aware that glass and aluminium could be recycled. I suggested that we collect glass and aluminium for a week and see how much accumulated. As the school had no kitchen, and all the children had to bring a picnic lunch, the amount was considerable (sandwiches came wrapped in foil and some children brought yoghurt in glass containers). That Friday, we took a trip to the local bottle bank to drop off our 'recyclables'; most of the children had seen such bins before, but none had known what they were for.

Upon returning, the children decorated a box which they kept near the rubbish bin for the collection of glass and aluminium. They also deposited any bits of foil they found littering the playground. This led someone to ask why the older children did not recycle their own rubbish. Another child suggested, 'Maybe they don't have a box.' Still another suggested making a recycling box for every class. Thus the whole school project was born.

The children counted how many classes there were in the school, and we gathered cardboard cartons from the supermarket. The children insisted that the cartons had to be brightly painted so that others would find them attractive and want them in their class; several days were spent on group box-painting. We then planned another assembly. The children displayed their large collages and told about their visit to the bottle bank. I showed slides I had taken of the children putting the coloured glass and aluminium into the correct bins. The children then asked each class to take away a recycling box.

The children were enormously pleased with their assembly – except for the fact that two classes did not take a box. The children found it difficult to understand that not everyone would share their enthusiasm for the project; it was a hard lesson in the reality that not everyone is willing to make an effort on behalf of the environment.

Nonetheless, the project went on. Each Friday for the remainder of the school year, four children were chosen on a rota basis to go from classroom to classroom with a wagon, collecting all the glass and aluminium, which they then took to the bottle bank. Their enthusiasm for the project never lagged. We re-read *Dinosaurs and All That Rubbish* several times, as well as *The Lorax* by Dr. Seuss (Collins, London, 1971), which helped to keep their interest high. We made lists of foods that came in aluminium packaging and graphed the number of products that came in clear, green and brown glass bottles and jars. Regrettably, the actual centre where the glass was re-processed was over two hours away by bus, too far for a visit.

To my surprise, I got a lot of parent feedback – most of it initially negative. Parents came to school complaining that their children were reprimanding them when they threw away glass jars or aluminium cans at home, and telling them to take them to recycling bins instead. Many parents were not willing to go to the trouble to do so and found their children's insistence quite annoying. One threatened to start bringing her household rubbish into school if I kept on with the project! Over time, however, even the more negative parents admitted that their children were in fact acquiring important attitudes towards the environment.

While I did not manage to tackle the question of what to do with all the recyclable paper that gets thrown away each day, I am looking into linking with a local secondary school that has a paper recycling project. My children really had the sense that they were doing something important as a result of this experience, and that would only be heightened by contact with older children who are involved in providing a similar kind of service.'

Putting discussion and communication skills to a practical end, co-operating to create a positive outcome that benefits self and others, becoming aware that there are a variety of points of view on any issue and, above all, realising that one's efforts can produce change – these are among the potential areas of learning that can arise through an appropriate action project. Other possible projects might include:

- Planting trees in the school grounds or on nearby wasteland
- Creating a wildlife garden near the school grounds
- Looking at classroom arrangement and making changes that will improve the range of activities provided
- Examining what children actually do in the school playground and making recommendations to the rest of the school about types of activities or equipment that would make it more interesting
- Making a safety survey of the school building and the surrounding area, with recommendations for improvements
- Fundraising through used toy exchanges, jumble sales, cake sales, in order to make a financial contribution towards improvements which children might suggest as a result of studying their school or local environment
- Older infants can work in nursery classes – reading, assisting in craft projects, participating in playground games – as a way both of developing sensitivity to the needs of younger children, and of recognising their own progressive growth and development
- Forming a link with an organisation or institution which serves the elderly, sharing visits or celebrating holidays with them
- Linking with a school which serves handicapped children to exchange visits, share project work, or take joint field trips to places of mutual interest
- Linking with a school from a different type of local environment, i.e. city and rural, inner city and suburban, to share typical school experiences and to enlarge perspectives on how school life may vary within the same town
- Linking with a school in a developing country to exchange photographs, letters and information about daily school life.

Whole-school Implications

Relationships between members of the teaching staff should ideally reflect an atmosphere of co-operation.

Teaching in many primary schools takes place in isolated individual classrooms. Teachers who work with children in affirming, interactive and co-operative ways often become aware of the implications of how staff members relate to each other as well, and may begin to look at ways of working together to overcome physical barriers between classrooms. Co-operation between staff members can take many forms: the sharing of ideas and materials; co-operation in planning projects; exchanging time between classes so that teachers may share particular skills or points of view; observing colleagues trying out new techniques and offering feedback; joining classes for certain activities or special events; teaching as a team; making goal-setting decisions during staff meetings. As teachers begin to implement co-operative practices which break down their sense of isolation, a common experience seems to be that their own self-esteem is raised. As they share ideas and resources, they feel positive about the ways in which they are increasing their effectiveness. Exchanging feedback on children or teaching techniques extends those positive feelings. Sharing an awareness of each other's problems can reduce the demoralising feeling of being the only one who is not coping with a particular type of difficulty, a frequent experience particularly for young teachers or those new to a school. Furthermore, co-operative working relationships between adults model in a non-verbal way the type of behaviour that is being encouraged in the children.

A degree of devolution of authority may take place, so that there is an increased staff input into decision-making.

Just as teachers who develop co-operative approaches to learning may begin to relinquish some of their role as an ultimate authority over the children in their classes, the sharing of some decision-making power *among* adults in the school is also a logical outcome of the implementation of co-operative relationships between staff members. Teachers may find that they wish to be involved in decision-making on a deeper level – setting agendas for in-service work, running staff meetings collectively, writing or re-writing school policy documents, or examining traditions such as holiday assemblies, awards assemblies or sports days to see if they contain underlying implications that may need changing. Such involvement may be accompanied by increased responsibilities, as well as an increased sense of commitment and 'ownership'. Headteachers need to be aware of the implications for their roles, which may shift from that of 'leading' (as traditionally conceptualised) to that of 'facilitating' the growth and development of children, teachers and programmes within a school.

'I've been working for several years now to try to get the staff to build self-esteem and co-operation in the children. But I have to carry that through to the staff meetings as well. I can't just go in there and dictate to them what the topic of the next training day is going to be, or how we're going to raise funds, because that would be hypocritical. I have to give them time to say what they feel and want. But with the climate of trust that we've been building up, it's amazing sometimes how quickly we can reach consensus. Teachers on this staff really like each other; you can feel it when you walk into the staffroom.'

A primary school headteacher.

Non-teaching staff can be recognised for the significant impact they have on children's lives.

When school life is designed to encourage self-esteem, communication and co-operation, it is inclusive of *all* members of staff, and does not marginalise non-teaching members of the school community. Schools in which such an approach is taken seriously inevitably come to recognise the impact that classroom assistants, language support staff, kitchen staff, dinner and playground supervisors and caretakers have on the children. These schools may also explore ways to help these staff members feel more a part of the educational environment. Some schools have tried creating displays in the entrance hall with photographs of *all* the adults who work there, with affirming statements about their contributions. Other schools have attempted to offer introductory training for non-teaching staff on the impact of self-esteem, communication and co-operation upon teacher–child and child–child relationships; some have provided workshops for playground supervisors on co-operative games for children.

An educational home visitor in an inner-city school was concerned about how little there was for children to do in the playground, and the problems with children's behaviour that were occurring there. She decided to research children's games from a variety of cultures. When she had gathered together a small collection of these games, she began teaching them to the playground supervisors. She asked them to teach some of the games to the children, and to complete evaluation sheets, rating how well each game had been received.

She found that the interest among the playground supervisors was high; they were pleased to have a new skill to share with the children, and to have their opinions on the various games sought out. A change in attitude on the part of the children was noted as well: 'The games project has raised the status of the playground supervisors in the children's eyes. They now realise that they are people who have something constructive to offer, and the children relate to them with more respect.'

Despite the problems of finding time and financial resources for such initiatives, a continued exploration of ways in which to involve non-teaching staff creatively could have a far-reaching impact in schools which wish truly to embody an attitude of respect for each individual's input, to encourage open communication between members of the school community and to provide a model of co-operative interaction.

Parent education can become an important means of developing support for the aims of the school.

The importance of educating parents about the implications of global education for young children is increasingly being recognised. Nursery and infant teachers, who traditionally have more contact with parents than teachers of middle or secondary school students, tend to see clearly the link between the parents' ways of relating to their children and the behaviour and attitudes of these children towards others later on in life. Teachers of young children often sense that a greater awareness in the home of the role of affirmation, effective communication and co-operation on children's development could be an invaluable support to the work that goes on in school. Many teachers have tried holding parents' meetings to share information on their classroom approaches; some have included workshop sessions in which parents can experience interactive learning strategies first-hand and discuss their own personal reactions.

A reception class teacher comments on using **Co-operative Squares** (page 70) at a parents' meeting:

'It was fascinating to watch the different reactions; one group found it easy to work together and solved the problem quickly. One person in another group got so competitive and frustrated by the whole experience that she took all the pieces from everyone in the group and tried to figure it out on her own. (Her son often does the same sort of thing in class!) At the end, though, everyone agreed that it had been a useful experience. Many expressed surprise that the school was trying to develop social skills like co-operation – they had no idea that sort of thing went on, but they were really quite pleased about it. One parent left saying she had noticed her son being more helpful at home since he started in my class, and that now she understood why.

Several of the parents said how much fun they had had at this meeting – one said she wished she had tape-recorded it so that she could play it for her husband, who hadn't come to that evening. Maybe using activities like this more often would encourage a better turn-out at parents' meetings!'

Devising ways of effectively communicating to parents the ideas behind global education in the infant school is as yet an emerging area, but one which could potentially multiply the benefits of the school-based approach.

In-service training is vital to the implementation of a whole-school approach to global education.

Putting the type of whole-school approach described above into practice requires a high level of trust, communication and co-operation between staff. Such relationships do not simply 'happen' without a conscious commitment on the part of the staff to the on-going process of interpersonal understanding. Some schools may decide that a certain amount of time during staff meetings needs to be devoted to this process, or that honest and effective communication may be an area to explore during in-service training. In the zeal with which such an initiative is sometimes undertaken, it must be remembered that individuals will vary widely in their ability to trust others, express ideas and feelings openly and work collaboratively. Acceptance of, and respect for, such individual differences forms the foundation for the building of a co-operative teaching team in which each member feels valued.

A highly practical orientation to in-service training is essential in order to put into practice work of the type described in this book. Awareness of effective ways of supporting the growth of children's self-esteem will be heightened by exercises in which teachers themselves give and receive affirmation. Experiences which allow them to examine their own ways of communicating, and which put them in situations requiring co-operation with others in order to complete tasks, will likewise bring to the surface a range of thoughts and feelings on the problems and potential of such work in the classroom. Time must be allowed for debriefing and exploring the implications of the various activities. Just as importantly, training sessions should be structured to give teachers a chance to get to know each other as people and to build a sense of safety and trust within the group.

Below is a sample programme for a 'taster' day on self-esteem, communication and co-operation for teachers of children under seven. Though any of these three areas could be the topic of a full day (or longer) workshop, the programme below is intended to be an introduction for teachers who have no experience of global education approaches in the nursery and infant school.

9:00   **Attribute Linking** (page 21)

9:10   **Affirmation Badges** (page 22)

9:25   Input: Outline of the day. What are the foundations of global education for 4–7-year-olds?

9:45   Brainstorm in small groups: What are characteristics of a child with positive self-esteem? With low self-esteem? Plenary discussion.

10:10   Input on self-esteem research.

10:20   **Affirmation on Paper** (page 25). Debriefing.

10:50   Coffee.

11:10   **Police Officer, Have You Seen My Friend?** (page 25)

11:20   Self-esteem role-plays:

91

    a A child shows her painting to the teacher; the teacher responds with lavish praise.

    b A child shows her Lego® model to the teacher; the teacher responds in an affirming way but without using any adjectives.

Small group discussion of **a** and **b.**

    c Two children fight over a pencil; the teacher settles the argument and gets the children back to work.

    d Two children fight over their place in line; the teacher helps the children to find a solution without making any suggestions of her own.

Small group discussion of **c** and **d.**

    e A child who has been doing sums brings them to the teacher, saying, 'That was easy for me!' The teacher sees that half of them are incorrect. She responds . . .

Plenary discussion of role-plays.

12:00 Input on communication skills.

12:10 **Interviews** (page 21) in pairs on the topic 'A significant school experience that affected my self-esteem as a child was . . . ' Reporting back in groups of six.

12:35 **Overloading** (page 39) on the topic 'I feel supported at work when . . . '

12:40 **Bean Discussion** (page 48) on the topic 'My reactions to the training day so far . . . '

12:55 **Minute of Silence** (page 44).

13:00 Lunch.

14:00 **Going Dotty** (page 45). Debriefing.

14:10 **Co-operative Squares** (page 70). Debriefing, discussion of **Modified Co-operative Squares** (page 71), **Co-operative Circles** (page 72) and **Co-operative Faces** (page 73).

14:45 Input on research on co-operative learning.

15:00 **Lock and Key** (page 58).

15:05 **Cars and Drivers** (page 55) with partner from **Lock and Key.** Debriefing in pairs, then as a whole group.

15:30 Tea.

15:45 Board games session: in groups of six, teachers spend ten minutes playing and discussing a co-operative board game (pages 60–70). Groups then rotate and spend ten minutes with a different board game. Plenary discussion on potential of co-operative board games.

16:25 Small group discussion: In order to implement an ethos of self-esteem, open communication and co-operation in our school, what changes would need to be made? Consider change on a variety of levels: personal, interpersonal, curriculum, structuring of time and space, administrative, in-service training. Reporting back from groups and plenary.

         17:00 Close.

Comments from participants after in-service training sessions on the foundations of global education for four- to seven-year-olds:

'After attending the workshop I felt challenged and stimulated by the examples I had been presented with. The children need this kind of learning built into their curriculum. They already seem to have plenty of opportunity to be competitive. The role of the teacher is to awaken in children a consciousness of others.'

A teacher of seven-year-olds.

'I do not usually enjoy partaking in practical workshop experiences, but this proved to be the exception.'

A teacher of five-year-olds.

'It has been really valuable in terms of getting to know staff and becoming more relaxed and open with them. Ideas and adaptations for my class are already coming to mind. I hope it has a long-term effect. Anyway, I realise now that it has to be a consistent, continual approach with the children. Some of the co-operative activities (like the squares) could be approached in a competitive way.'

A teacher of six-year-olds.

'I particularly enjoyed the way the day was organised in a practical way. I find that 'doing' is so much more effective than just listening to someone pontificate. However, I do think that we tried to cover so much and we had to cut short sessions which really could have gone on and been beneficial.'

A teacher of five-year-olds.

'The simplicity of technique and use of readily available resources make this important and exciting work accessible to all class teachers. More importantly, I was struck by the depth of the discussion that the workshop provoked. Teachers were speaking so personally – about their own philosophies of education, about childhood experiences that had shaped them – I learned things about staff that I hadn't discovered in my previous three years of working with them. This is the level of discussion we should be having at all our staff meetings!'

A primary school headteacher.

'It really changed my objectives – I now think it's extremely important to let the children learn at their own pace. I now finally understand the difference between games that are just non-competitive and games which are truly co-operative. I think both have their place, but now I can be clearer about exactly what I'm doing and why. Also, it's important to plan a sequence of activities to help children grasp the message, rather than do it just once and drop it.'

A teacher of three-year-olds.

'The biggest change for me coming out of the workshop was that it modified the way I organised my parent meeting. I tried using some co-operative activities with them, actually placing them in a position of problem-solving in a small group, then coming together as a big

93

group to discuss it. The parents were fascinated by the idea that these activities could build both cognitive skills and social skills at the same time. It takes a lot of courage – the first time I did it I was panicking! It's not an easy way, but it's a much more dynamic, creative way of running your meeting – because you can't predict the outcome of the meeting. You have to be quite flexible and accept that you are guiding it, but you can't determine what's coming out.

I'm going to try again and again – because it's worth it! And I'll get better at it!'

A teacher of four-year-olds.

References

1   See for example Rosenthal, R. and Jacobson, L., *Pygmalion in the Classroom* (Holt Rinehart & Winston, New York, 1968); Rist, R. C., 'Student social class and teacher expectations: the self-fulfilling prophecy in ghetto education' in *Harvard Educational Review*, Vol. 40, No. 3 (August 1970); Rubovits and Maehr, 'Pygmalion black and white', *Journal of Personality and Social Psychology*, Vol. 25, No. 2 (1973) pp. 210–18.

2   Staub, E., 'To Rear a Prosocial Child: Reasoning, Learning by Doing, and Learning by Teaching Others', in DePalma, D. and Foley, J., (eds), *Moral Development: Current Theory and Research* (Lawrence Erlbaum Associates, New Jersey, 1975).

BIBLIOGRAPHY

Background Reading on Global Education and Child Development

Davey, A., *Learning to be Prejudiced* (Edward Arnold, London, 1983). Research on the ways prejudice develops; conclusions on the role of co-operation in the classroom, relevant for teachers of young children.

Ferguson, M., *The Aquarian Conspiracy* (Granada, London, 1980). An exploration of the emergence of a changing concept of human potential and its implications for Western culture.

Greig, S., Pike, G. and Selby, D., *Earthrights* (The WWF and Kogan Page, London, 1987). A short, readable overview of current global problems and trends and the response of global education.

Hanvey, R. G., *An Attainable Global Perspective*, Global Perspectives in Education (New York, 1982). A useful pamphlet which describes five critical elements of education for a global perspective.

Hazareesingh, S., Simms, K. and Anderson, P., *Educating the Whole Child* (Building Blocks Educational, 1989). A holistic approach to education for under-fives which examines the influence of race, class and gender differences.

Johnson, D. W. and Johnson, R. T., *Learning Together and Alone* (Prentice Hall, New Jersey, 1975). Research findings on co-operative, competitive and individualised learning strategies.

Johnson, D. W. and Johnson, R. T., *The Socialization and Achievement Crisis: Are Co-operative Learning Experiences the Solution?* (Sage Publications, 1983). A further exploration of research into co-operative learning.

Lawrence, D., *Enhancing Self-esteem in the Classroom* (Paul Chapman Press, London, 1987). An excellent review of research on self-esteem and its impact on social and academic progress.

Mussen, P. and Eisenberg-Berg, N., *Roots of Caring, Sharing, and Helping* (W. H. Freeman, San Francisco, 1977). A fascinating volume reviewing research on the origins of prosocial behaviour, specifically dealing with nursery and infant children.

Pike, G. and Selby, D., *Global Teacher, Global Learner* (Hodder and Stoughton, London, 1988). A definitive handbook for teachers, developing the theory and practice of global education, and offering a range of practical activities for primary and secondary classrooms.

Rogers, C., *Freedom to Learn for the 80's* (Charles E. Merrill, Columbus, Ohio, 1983). An inspirational book on person-centred learning, with an important chapter on research findings.

95

Spivack, G. and Shure, M., *Social Adjustment of Young Children* (Jossey-Bass, San Francisco, 1976). A detailed outline of a conflict-resolution training programme which, while somewhat didactic, is easily adaptable for the nursery–infant classroom.

Practical Handbooks and Classroom Resources

Anderson, P., Hazareesingh, S. and Simms, K., *Through My Windows: Storytelling Pack* (Building Blocks Educational, 1989). The pack includes excellent teacher guidelines for using stories in the multicultural classroom, as well as two multi-ethnic children's books, visual aids, a cassette recording of one of the books (available in five South Asian languages) and songs which accompany the books.

Birmingham Development Education Centre, *Get the Picture* (1989). A handbook of ideas for developing skills of interpreting visual images in infant children.

Birmingham Development Education Centre, *Working Now* (1988). This outstanding multi-ethnic collection of photos shows women and men in a variety of non-gender-stereotyped occupations.

Borba, M. and Borba, C., *Self-esteem: A Classroom Affair* (Winston Press, Minneapolis, 1978). Lots of ideas for activities which enhance self-esteem, geared to the primary school.

Borba, M. and Borba, C., *Self-esteem: A Classroom Affair: Vol. 2* (Winston Press, Minneapolis, 1982). A further collection of affirming techniques and ideas.

Brandes, D. and Phillips, H., *Gamesters' Handbook* (Hutchinson, London, 1977). A useful source of co-operative, interactive techniques, some of which can be adapted for nursery and infant children.

Brandes, D., *Gamesters' Handbook Two* (Hutchinson, London, 1982). More co-operative activities, similar to volume 1.

Canfield, J. and Wells, H., *100 Ways to Enhance Self-concept in the Classroom* (Prentice Hall, New Jersey, 1976). Imaginative ideas for fostering self-esteem; geared to older primary/secondary children, but some ideas are adaptable to the early years.

Fisher, S. and Hicks, D. W., *World Studies 8–13. A Teacher's Handbook* (Oliver and Boyd, 1985). While designed for top junior/secondary students, it provides a useful overview of the topics and techniques of world studies.

Fountain, S., *Helping Hands* and *Haunted House* (1990).

Hendricks, G. and Wills, R., *The Centering Book* (Prentice Hall, New Jersey, 1975). A useful collection of approaches to relaxation, visualisation and focusing awareness; with some adaptations, they can be used with younger children.

Hendricks, G. and Roberts, T. B., *The Second Centering Book* (Prentice Hall, New Jersey, 1977). More centring activities.

Judson, S., *A Manual on Non-violence and Children* (New Society Publishers, Philadelphia, 1977). An excellent source of co-operative activities and ideas on conflict resolution, with a section on nursery children.

Liebmann, M., *Art Games and Structures for Groups: A Handbook of Themes, Games and Exercises* (Croom Helm, 1986). Interesting ideas for using art to facilitate co-operation and self-awareness.

Maidenhead Teachers' Centre, *Doing Things* (Trentham Books, 1987). An excellent multi-ethnic photo pack showing girls and boys, women and men in a variety of traditional and non-traditional roles in the home. The teacher's guide offers numerous suggestions for ways of using the photos.

Masheder, M., *Let's Co-operate,* Peace Education Project. A lively collection of ideas for encouraging self-esteem, communication and co-operation, many of which are appropriate for the nursery–infant age range.

Newcastle upon Tyne L.E.A., *Co-operating for a Change* (1987). Compiled by a group of teachers in the Walker district of Newcastle, this handbook offers a wide range of co-operative activities for the primary school, with evaluations by the teachers.

Orlick, T., *The Co-operative Sports and Games Book* (Writers and Readers Publishing Co-operative, London, 1978). A superb source of co-operative games for the hall or the classroom, including games from other cultures, and a section on games for children under seven.

Orlick, T., *The Second Co-operative Sports and Games Book* (Pantheon, New York, 1982). A further collection of games for all ages, including a chapter on co-operative approaches for children under three.

Pax Christi, *Winners All* (Stanhope Press, London, 1980). A small but useful collection of co-operative games, some of which are appropriate for infants.

Philip & Tacey, North Way, Andover, Hants, SP10 5BA. Two co-operative board games for 5–7-year-olds (see page 70).

Prutzman, P., Burger, M. L., Bodenhamer, G. and Stern, L., *The Friendly Classroom for a Small Planet* (Avery Publishing Group, New Jersey, 1978). An indispensible book of activities on self-esteem, communication, co-operation, role-play and conflict resolution, many of which can be used in early childhood classrooms.

Thomas, P., *Getting on with Others* (The Woodcraft Folk, London, 1988). A loose-leaf pack with activities to develop the notion of interdependence, and to begin exploring issues of racism and sexism with infants.

97

INDEX OF ACTIVITIES

Affirmation Badges   22
Affirmation Notebooks   29
Affirmation on Paper   25
Attribute Linking   21

Bean Discussions   48
Body Tracings   26
The Bridge Across   63
Building a House   65

Cars and Drivers   55
Class Web   53
Cooper Says   40
Co-operative Circles   72
Co-operative Faces   73
Co-operative Hot Potato   55
Co-operative Musical Hoops   50
Co-operative Musical Hugs   50
Co-operative Pin the Tail on the
    Donkey   57
Co-operative Squares   70
Co-operative Storytelling   46
Crowns and Statues   52

Doggie, Doggie, Where's Your
    Bone?   56

Escape from the Zoo   42

Farmyard   40
Feeling Sounds   23
Feelings Walk   23

Going Dotty   45

Human Chalkboards   39

I Hug Myself 'Cause I Love Me
    So!   34
Interviews   21
Introductory Name Game   20

Listen and Clap   41
Little Boy Blue   61
Lock and Key   58

Magic Microphone   47
The Magic Tree   60
Mask Passing   22
Minute of Silence   44
Modified Co-operative Squares   71
Musical Laps   49

Names in Motion   44
No Hands!   55

Overloading   39

The Park Game   67
Pass the Sound   41
Picturematch   59
Police Officer, Have You Seen My
    Friend?   25

The 'Seed' Visualisation   27
Shipwreck   57

Telegraph   38
Telephone   36
This is My Friend   20

Use Your Senses   45